1931

The Year of the Great Worldwide Financial Crash

Eric H. Allen

ii

Contents

List of Figures

List of Tables

Acknowledgements

The author would like to acknowledge several individuals who made particular contributions to this book:

Dan Blatt, publisher of FUTURECASTS on-line magazine (available at www.futurecasts.com), who proofread the manuscript and offered many helpful comments and corrections;

Robert E. Emerson and my brother, Scott O. Allen, who produced a professional quality book cover on short notice;

Donald Knuth, Leslie Lamport, and the other contributors to TeX and LaTeX, who developed a document preparation system that remains as functional, useful, and reliable today as when it was first introduced over 25 years ago;

My thesis advisor, Dr. Marija Ilić, now at Carnegie Mellon University, who has provided much sage advice in bringing this project to fruition and vouched for the skills of the author;

My parents, Owen F. and Candace H. Allen, and my sister, Deborah L. Allen, who have encouraged and supported this project throughout;

God, for all of the gifts He has given me that made this book possible.

Preface

The 2008 financial crisis prompted much talk about "preventing a repeat of the Great Depression" and justification of drastic actions to that end. The subsequent events of 2008-09, however, bear an eerie resemblance to the way the depression unfolded during 1929-30 – *because of*, not despite, these drastic policies. A historical review of the Great Depression shows that the events of 1931 were far more significant than those of 1929. 1931 was truly the year when lifestyles began to be affected by the depression on a broad scale [5, p. 146].

These factors prompted the writing of this book – to concisely explain the monetary and economic developments that made 1931 such a significant year, to collect in one place a description of the combination of factors that culminated in the 1931 monetary collapse and ensuing Great Depression, and to show the similarities – and differences – between then and now. Contemporary financial data is presented throughout to illustrate the events that occurred. The events are presented principally from a United States perspective, but key international events and statistics are included as well.

The Great Depression produced widespread suffering throughout the world. It demands serious analysis and examination, not a flippant "oh, capitalism is unstable!" response. It is a goal of this book to improve understanding of money, banking, and the role both played in the 1931 global financial crisis and subsequent Great Depression. It is also hoped that this book can aid in preventing the same mistakes from being repeated in the future.

Chapter 1

Introduction

The Great Depression was undoubtedly the most traumatic economic event to date in American history. The stock market crash etched the year 1929 into the public's mind as the beginning of the historic depression, yet few people today are aware of the much larger financial convulsions that shook the world two years later. It wasn't until after these events - repudiation of monetary commitments by governments around the world, the worst month in stock market history to date[1], a run on gold reserves in the U.S. - that the Depression truly became "Great."

1931 was a convergence point of many economic forces. Some of these forces had been building for over a decade, while others developed within the preceding year or two. The combination of a long-term economic contraction from the formation of trade barriers worldwide, various economic and political forces which had significantly distorted the economy, and an inherently unstable monetary system that amplified economic adjustments resulted in an enormous and devastating downward economic swing.

The forces that combined to produce the Great Depression can be classified into several categories:

1. Long-term Economic Impediments

   These forces created a semi-permanent reduction in worldwide economic output that could not be attributed to normal business cycle adjustments. They constituted setbacks and weights on economic growth that would remain in place even after transitional economic

---

[1]according to the Dow Jones Industrial Average [16] and the Standard and Poor 500 index [252]

adjustments were completed. Aside from the physical destruction of the Great War and the "Balkanization" of central Europe [36], [28] these drags on the overall economy were generally the result of legislated government policies that could only be reversed by repeal or amendment – a very difficult, time-consuming process, especially since the adverse impact of these policies was generally not evident to the governments that had enacted them.

(a) Worldwide trade protectionism [5]

(b) Development of socialism and statism, particularly in Europe [25, 40, 121, 186]

(c) Destruction of economic assets during World War I [5, p. 183]

2. Destabilizing Elements of the Economic Structure
   These elements were also government enactments and thus difficult to change, but unlike the first category, they did not directly impede economic activity but instead tended to amplify price swings and economic adjustments, magnifying the size of economic swings.

(a) Fractional reserve banking [41, 255]

(b) World War I debts and reparations [5]

(c) Extended period of inflationary money policy [41, 254]

3. Cyclical Economic Developments
   These factors recur in every business cycle, including the business cycle which peaked in 1929. The cyclical economic contraction that followed this peak then combined with the preceding factors to create a truly historic economic contraction.

(a) Obsolete methods of production [11]

(b) Malinvestments [254]

These elements were already in place prior to the 1929 stock market crash. They were, however, exacerbated by additional policies instituted in 1929 and 1930:

1. Commencement of Federal Farm Board price supports (1929) [5, 41, 254]

2. The Smoot-Hawley Tariff (1930) [5, 41, 254]

3. Hoover's policy of "encouraging" maintenance of wage rates [41, 254]

4. Expanded government spending [41, 254]

5. Historically cheap money policy [35, 41, 254]

Because of these additional policies, an economic downturn that might have stabilized in 1930 or early 1931 instead took a sharp turn for the worse as conditions deteriorated even further. The additional strain on the banking and monetary systems finally led to a loss of confidence in banks and the currency itself, precipitating the final collapse.

1.1   Business Cycles

Economic business cycles have been observed for centuries. Fundamentally, they are the inevitable result of the periodic accumulation of unproductive capital that occurs in a growing economy. Initially, growing economies produce more than they consume, with the excess being either invested or saved. Over time, however, as the economy becomes more prosperous, less productive businesses and practices develop and accumulate [5, p. 330]. Newer, more efficient production methods reduce the cost of producing certain goods, making older production techniques less valuable. Consumer tastes change over time, reducing the value of some goods. Some entrepreneurs, being human, misjudge consumers' desires and start businesses of dubious value [5, p. 336]. Eventually, the economy will begin to consume more than it produces. At that point, it is necessary for the unproductive capital to be liquidated in order to end the drain on the entire economy and free resources for future growth [11]. These periodic times of liquidation are depressions (or, in 20th century terminology, recessions).

Rising prices, especially for raw materials relative to finished products, consumer prices relative to wages, and imports relative to exports, are signals that the economy is consuming more than it is producing. Recessions are a consequence of the time lags that invariably exist in the pricing mechanisms. Prices can not instantly show the effect of the collective addition of many unproductive activities; only some time after these activities are under way will prices reflect their impact. These rising prices will initiate a series of liquidations as unproductive businesses become unprofitable and go bankrupt. Wasteful practices within otherwise productive businesses will also be trimmed. The consequent drop in consumption relative to production, along with the desire of the public to hold more cash[2], reverses the price increases soon afterward [254, pp. 15-16].

It is therefore seen that price inflation and recession are both symptoms of the same economic problem – consumption in excess of production. In fact, recession is actually a "healthier" condition than price inflation, because the "disease" – a burden of wasteful, inefficient, and unproductive activities – is being treated.

It should be noted that "unproductive" does not necessarily mean "lazy" or "slothful." Unproductive simply means that the goods produced are of little value in exchange. A person may in fact work very hard yet be unproductive – for example, a man who makes a 2 × 4 from a tree in his backyard will certainly expend much labor and time, but the final product is of comparatively little value, since machines can and do routinely make large quantities of the same product at little cost.

No one can deny that recessions and depressions are periods of much hardship for many. However, for workers in unproductive industries, there really is no alternative to either drastic wage cuts or layoffs. Government subsidies or other means to artificially sustain these businesses will only prolong the burden on the entire economy and all of the other members of society.[3] Old capital needs to be liquidated in order to make new capital available. Allowing the necessary wage cuts and bankruptcies to take place is the quickest means of ending the burden on the economy and society and restoring economic growth, which provides new job opportunities for displaced workers [254, pp. 14, 19-22], [11].

1.2   Gold Standard

As of 1900, United States currency was defined as a specified weight of gold. The Gold Standard Act of 1900 stated that a dollar was 25.8 grains of gold of .900 fineness [1, p. 144]. Therefore, one troy ounce[4] of gold was equal to $20.67. (Some people state that the gold price was "fixed" at $20.67, but this is an inaccurate statement. The gold price was not "fixed;" rather,

---

[2]Often dubbed a "decline in the velocity of money," [1, p. 292] this increased desire for cash is a natural reaction to economic uncertainty.

[3]The means of providing a "safety net" for workers during such job transitions has long been a difficult question. The only contention in this book is that such aid must not subsidize idleness and be a long-term drag on the overall economy.

[4]1 troy oz. = 480 grains

the legally recognized currency was gold [consistent with Article I Section 10 of the U.S. Constitution[5]], and a specific weight of gold was termed a "dollar." [255, pp. 30-32]) The Gold Standard Act of 1900 resolved the 19th century debates over a bimetallic system that attempted to establish a fixed value ratio between gold and silver that was contrary to the market valuations of the two metals [21, pp. 89-134].

1.3   Fractional Reserve Banking

The gold standard was undermined, however, by the widespread practice of fractional reserve banking. This banking system allows depositors to loan out a large portion of their deposited money while simultaneously being able to reclaim the same money, in full, on demand. Money is promised to the depositor at the same time it is already loaned out [255, pp. 51-60].

This practice results in more money in circulation than the actual monetary gold stock. Therefore, with fractional reserve banking, paper money is *always* present, even if a gold standard or silver standard is in place. As Ayn Rand eloquently stated: "Gold was an objective value, an equivalent of wealth produced. Paper is a mortgage on wealth that does not exist, ..." [251, p. 413]

Under fractional reserve banking, deposits and currency are mostly backed by loans and loan collateral instead of gold [24]. The loans and collateral are usually greater in value than gold at the time the loans are made (otherwise the loans likely wouldn't be made), but the true valuation of this debt changes over time. Convertibility of the paper currency into gold, however, attempts to equate the value of debt to gold, even though the true values may be significantly different.

Because the process of fractional reserve banking can be repeated multiple times as loaned money is deposited in other banks, the money supply expands during an economic expansion. During a depression, however, the process goes in reverse, causing the money supply to shrink. Usually, the shrinking process occurs much faster than the expansion [21, pp. 346].

As with any monetary inflation, prices are higher than they would be if the money supply were strictly limited to the existing gold stock. This inflation has corrosive effects on the economy. There is a time lag between the monetary inflation from the banking system and its impact on prices.

---

[5]Article I, Section 10: "No State shall ... make any Thing but gold and silver Coin a Tender in Payment of Debts"

This time lag from inflation adds to the natural time lags in the pricing mechanisms, allowing longer periods of accumulation of unproductive capital, thus amplifying the business cycle and creating larger booms and busts (depressions). The swings in the size of the money supply also greatly amplify the price swings associated with the business cycle [8], [5, p. 344].

The fractional reserve system is the fundamental reason that every recession in the 19th century was accompanied by bank panics and runs. A long-term economic contraction can collapse the value of the debt that is backing the currency in a fractional reserve system. If this should happen, there will naturally be a run on any available gold. After the Panic of 1907, the Federal Reserve System was created to provide a "lender of last resort" of liquidity – hard cash – to banks that were short of hard cash (i.e. gold) [21, pp. 168-171]. The root cause of the problem – fractional reserve banking – however, remained in place.

Aside from the obvious instability of a banking system prone to runs during recessions, such a system produces gross inequities among depositors at the same bank, as some are able to recover their deposits in full while others partially or completely lose their money.[6] This inequity arises solely because some people happen to be first in line when a bank run commences. Spreading losses among all depositors at the same bank is far more equitable. The system is akin to a giant Ponzi scheme[7].

> *"Whenever destroyers appear among men, they start by destroying money, for money is men's protection and the base of a moral existence. Destroyers seize gold and leave to its owners a counterfeit pile of paper. This kills all objective standards and delivers men into the arbitrary power of an arbitrary setter of values. Gold was an objective value, an equivalent of wealth produced. Paper is a mortgage on wealth that does not exist, backed by a gun aimed at those who are expected to produce it. Paper is a check drawn by legal looters upon an account which is not theirs: upon the virtue of the victims. Watch for the day when it bounces, marked: 'Account overdrawn.' "*

-Ayn Rand [251, p. 413]

---

[6]Deposit insurance only addresses this problem for individual banks, not the entire monetary system – see chapter 13.

[7]Ponzi scheme (n.) - "an investment swindle in which some early investors are paid off with money put up by later ones in order to encourage more and bigger risks" [38]

1.3.1 Money Supply

Throughout this book, three measures of the money supply – the number of dollars in existence – are presented: M_1, which includes currency in circulation and demand deposits in commercial banks[8]; M_2, which includes time deposits in commercial and mutual savings banks in addition to M_1[9]; and $M_{Rothbard}$, which includes building and loan deposits and cash surrender values of life insurance policies in addition to M_2 [254, pp. 87-91] (Figure 1.1). Since time deposits were, in practice, available on demand, the M_2 and $M_{Rothbard}$ measures provide better indications of the amount of claims that exist on the gold supply [254, pp. 87-91].

The ratio of the money supply to the gold stock is also presented throughout this book (Figure 1.3). The gold stock includes both bank holdings and gold coin in circulation [12] (Figure 1.2). (The Federal Reserve held all bank gold in the U.S. after 1917 [255, p. 81].) Under a true hard-money gold standard with 100% reserve banking, as advocated by Rothbard [255, pp. 159-186], this ratio[10] would always be 1.

1.3.2 Gold Flows

If gold coins were the only money in circulation, the gold would flow from nations with high prices to nations with low prices. The same thing happened with fractional reserve banking; nations with high prices would see their currency converted to gold, exported, and converted again into the currency of nations with low prices. Absent other economic factors, such gold movements would lead to falling prices in the gold exporting nations and rising prices in the gold importing nations. However, government desires to inflate currency and credit disrupted these gold movements and price dynamics. Gold flows would also follow the movement of loans and loan repayments.

---

[8]for the U.S., column 7 of Appendix A1 of [21]

[9]for the U.S., column 9 of Appendix A1 of [21]

[10]In theory, if the money supply/gold ratio is r, a long-term economic contraction of $1/(r-1)$ (e.g. a 10% contraction when the ratio of money to gold is 11) can devalue the debt backing the currency by an amount equal to the value of the entire gold stock. This is essentially what happened in 1931.

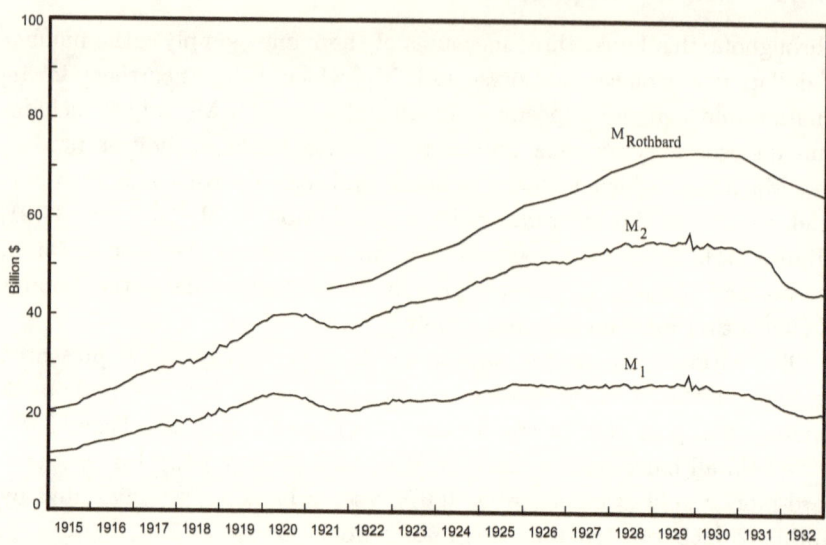

Figure 1.1: United States money supply, 1915 - 1932 [21]

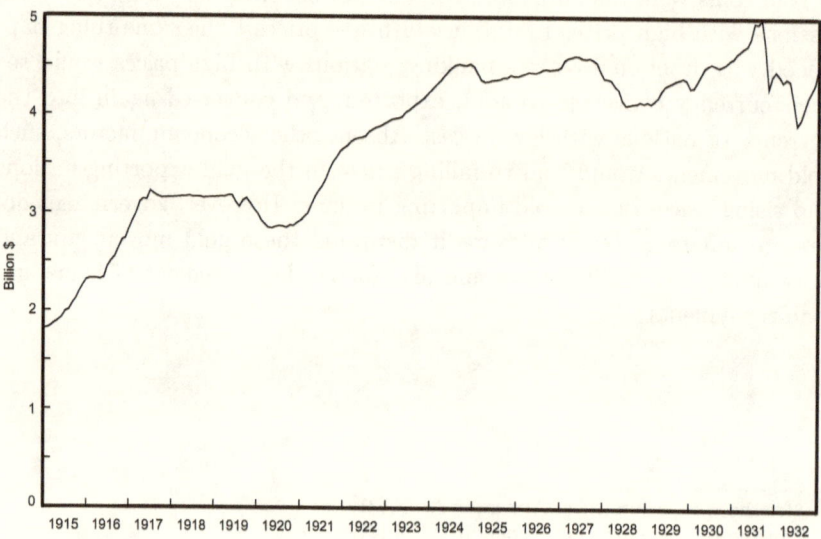

Figure 1.2: United States monetary gold stock, 1915 - 1932, including gold coin in circulation [12]

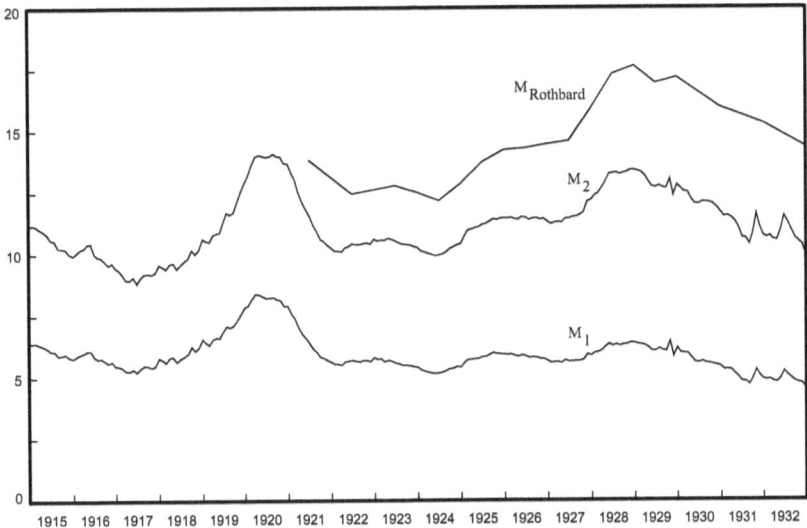

Figure 1.3: Ratio of money supply to monetary gold stock, 1915 - 1932

Chapter 2

1918-1923: Recovery from World War I

The physical destruction of World War I also meant economic destruction. Much productive capital was lost. The hostile feelings generated by the war, however, may well have been the most significant economic burden.

2.1   Treaty of Versailles

The Treaty of Versailles which formally ended World War I is widely regarded today as vindictive. (The Treaty of Brest Litovsk that Germany imposed on a defeated Russia in March 1918 was harsher, however.) Germany had little choice but to accept the Allies' terms, for Germany had been militarily defeated, and the Allies threatened to resume hostilities if a deadline of June 24, 1919 was not met. Four days later (June 28, 1919), the Treaty of Versailles was signed [256, pp. 57-59].

Germany was required to cede a number of parcels of land, including iron-rich Alsace-Lorraine [14] to France and Upper Silesia, an area with significant coal and steel production, to Poland. Other territorial concessions were made to Denmark and Belgium. Some of these concessions were conditioned on plebiscites. Germany was also required to virtually disarm [28], [256, pp. 57-59].

In direct financial penalties, the treaty imposed an initial reparations levy on Germany of 5 billion gold marks, equal to about 1.2 billion dollars.

Nation	Total War Debt (million $)	1913 National Product(million $)	Debt/Product Ratio
Belgium	418	1,300 (NNP)	32%
Britain	4,600	11,450 (GDP)	40%
France	4,025	8,753 (GDP)	46%
Italy	2,042	4,130 (GNP)	49%
Russia	193	N/A	N/A[1]
Others	480	-	-
Total	11,758	-	-

Table 2.1: War debts owed to United States after World War I [27]

The total reparations burden on Germany was fixed later (April 1921) at 132 billion marks, equal to about 31 billion dollars [256, p. 51]. This amount was about $2^1/_2$ times Germany's estimated pre-war NNP of 52.4 billion marks [39]. Germany had itself spent 164 billion marks on fighting the war; this money was raised by a combination of war loans (93 billion), Treasury bills (29 billion), and monetary inflation [256, p. 62].

The reparations levies were well in excess of Germany's gold holdings. The treaty thus specified goods that were to be provided by Germany in lieu of cash payments [256, p. 58].

2.2   War Debts

The warring nations borrowed heavily to finance the war. These debts were large, with a significant portion having been borrowed from the United States (see Table 2.1). The Allied nations in Europe wanted the German reparations payments to cover their war costs [28, 115].

2.3   Postwar Depression

Following the Great War, nations across the world endured economic depression as wartime industries were converted to peacetime production and monetary inflation was curtailed.

In the United States, a recession occurred from August 1918 to March 1919 as production transitioned from wartime to peacetime [21, pp. 221-

---

[1]After the Russian Revolution, the Bolsheviks refused to repay.

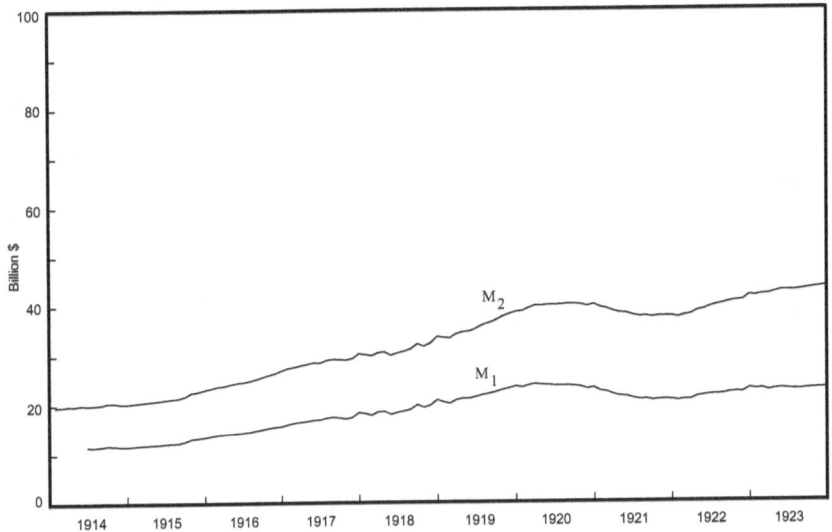

Figure 2.1: United States money supply, 1914 - 1923 [21]

222], [262]. Inflationary economic expansion then followed for the rest of the year as monetary policy remained loose (Figures 2.1 to 2.3). Driven by continued monetary expansion, prices continued to rise at a rate of about 14%/year, similar to the inflation rate during the war years of 1915-18 (Figure 2.4), but gold was no longer flowing in from abroad to support the monetary expansion as it had during the war. Tightening began quite abruptly at the end of the year. The discount rate[2] at the Federal Reserve Bank of New York jumped from 4% to 4.75% in December 1919, 6% in January 1920, and 7% in June 1920 (Figure 2.5), helping to bring the monetary expansion to an abrupt halt.

The ensuing depression in the United States produced a sharp rise in unemployment from 1.4% in 1919 to 11.7% in 1921 (Figure 2.6). GNP dropped 2.6% from 1920 to 1921 (Figure 2.7), but prices dropped 18% as measured by the GNP price deflator, and wholesale prices fell 36.8% in this period, the largest single year decline on record in the nation's history [262].

---

[2]The discount rate is the interest rate that a central bank charges commercial banks for borrowing money. The discount rate influences commercial bank interest rates and thus the amount of credit extended, which in turn influences the money supply. See [21, 32] for more details about central bank operations.

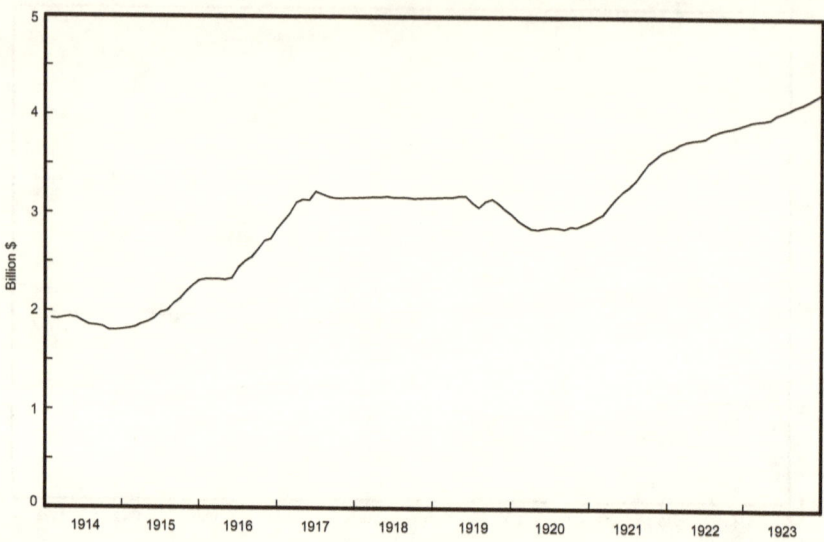

Figure 2.2: United States monetary gold stock, 1914 - 1923, including gold coin in circulation [12]

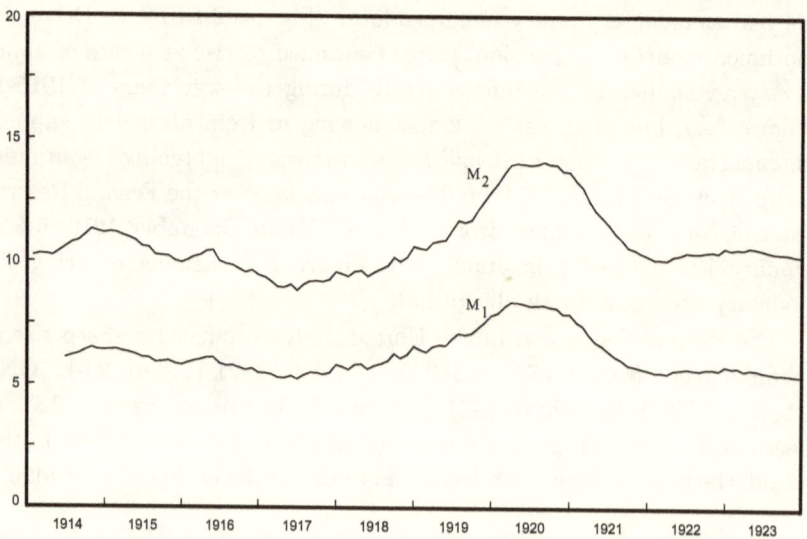

Figure 2.3: Ratio of money supply to monetary gold stock, 1914 - 1923

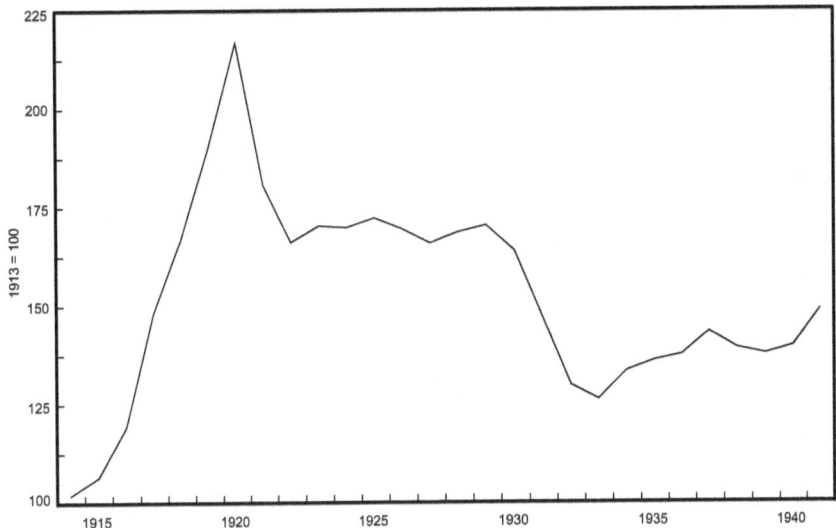

Figure 2.4: GNP price deflator index, 1914 - 1941 (1913 = 100) [29]

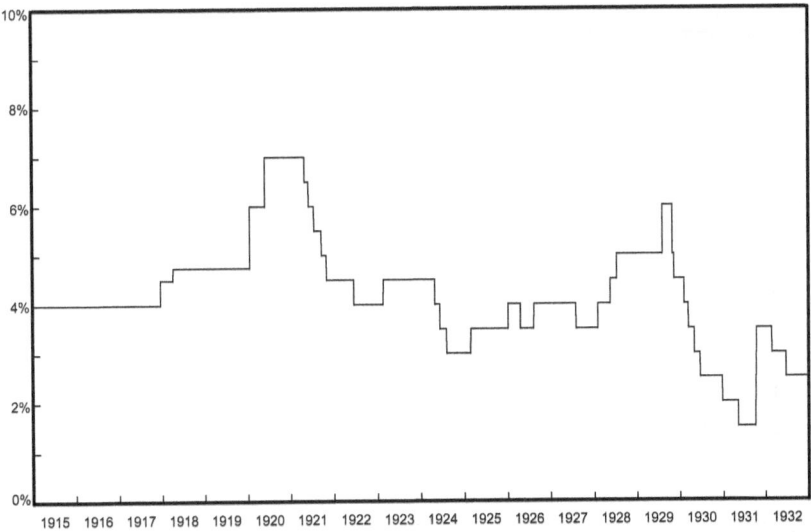

Figure 2.5: Discount rate of the New York Federal Reserve Bank, 1915 - 1932 [204, 232]

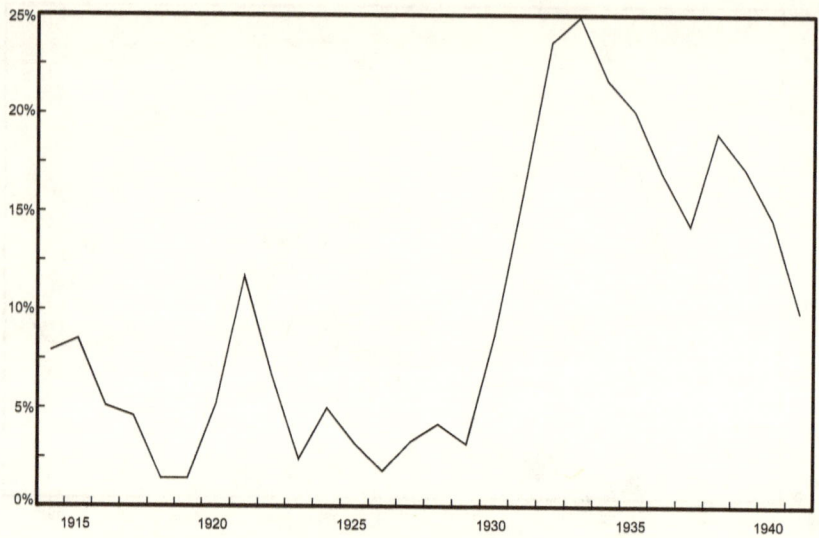

Figure 2.6: U.S. unemployment rate, 1914 - 1941 [29]

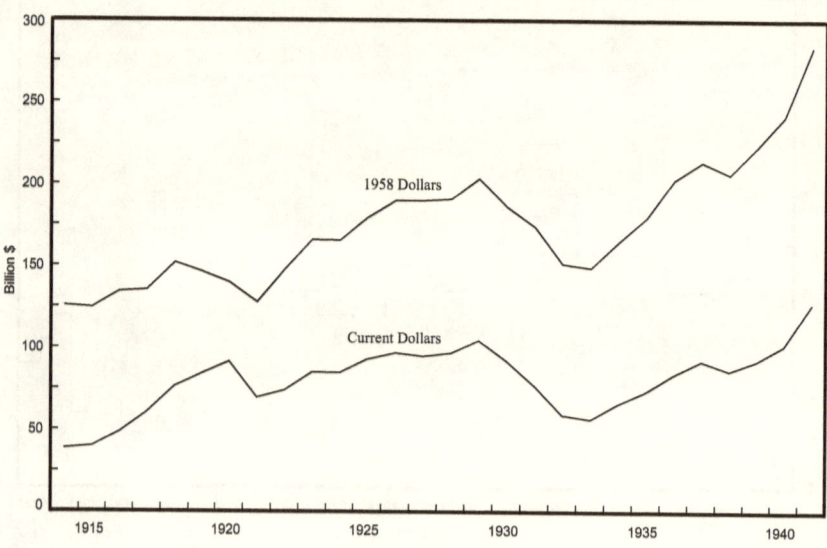

Figure 2.7: U.S. GNP in current and constant dollars, 1914 - 1941 [29]

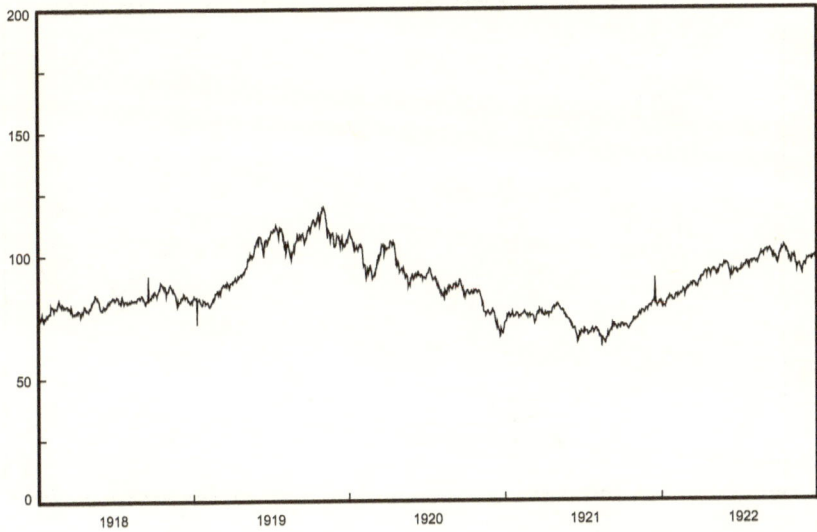

Figure 2.8: Dow Jones Industrial Average, 1918 - 1922 [16]

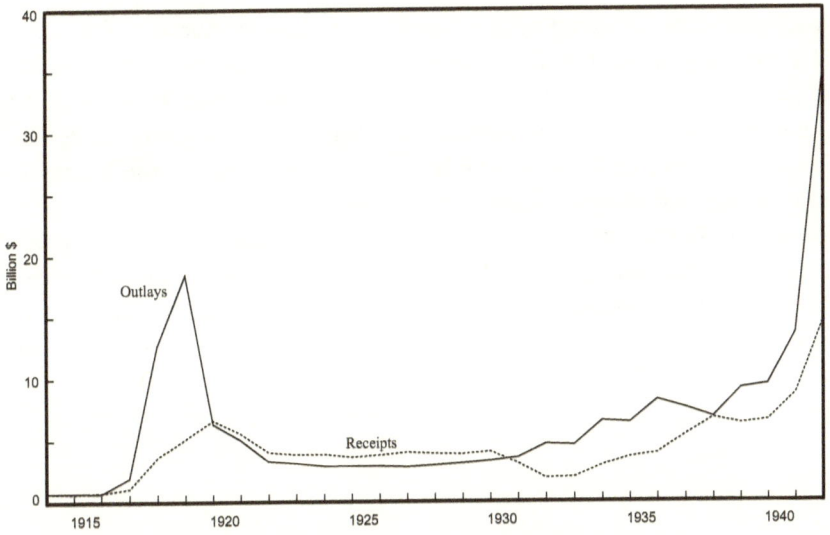

Figure 2.9: U.S. federal government outlays and receipts in current dollars, 1914 - 1941 [261]

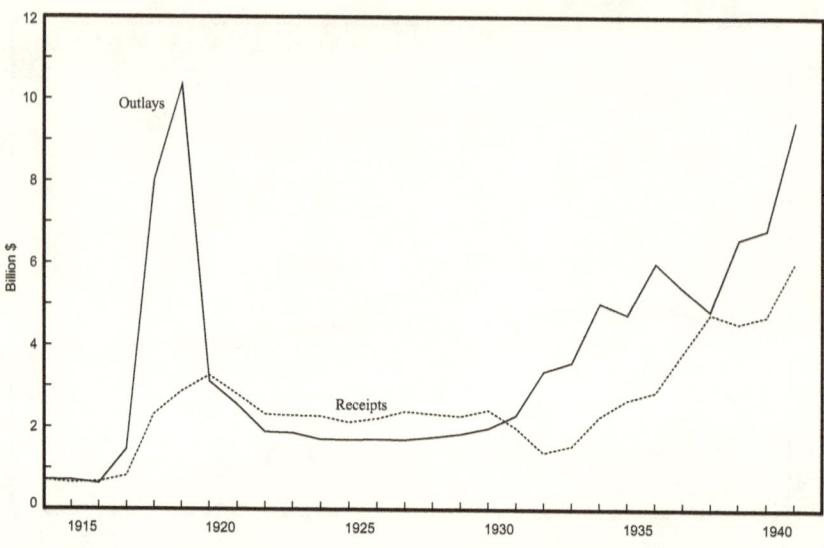

Figure 2.10: U.S. federal government outlays and receipts in 1913 dollars[3], 1914 - 1941

Stock prices, as measured by the Dow Jones Industrial Average (DJIA), fell 44% from a peak of 119.62 in November 1919 to 66.75 in December 1920 (Figure 2.8). With a long-standing gold standard, public expectations of deflation after the wartime inflation hastened the price drops [262]. The domestic agricultural sector was hit particularly hard by the depression and experienced especially large price drops as foreign agriculture started to recover after the war. Notable characteristics of this depression included a monetary tightening to curtail inflation – necessary for maintenance of the gold standard – a rapid increase in the labor force due to the return of service personnel from the war, a decline in exports, and large inventories of unsold goods [262], [5, p. 212].

---

[3]As calculated by GNP price deflator, averaged over two adjoining years for each fiscal year

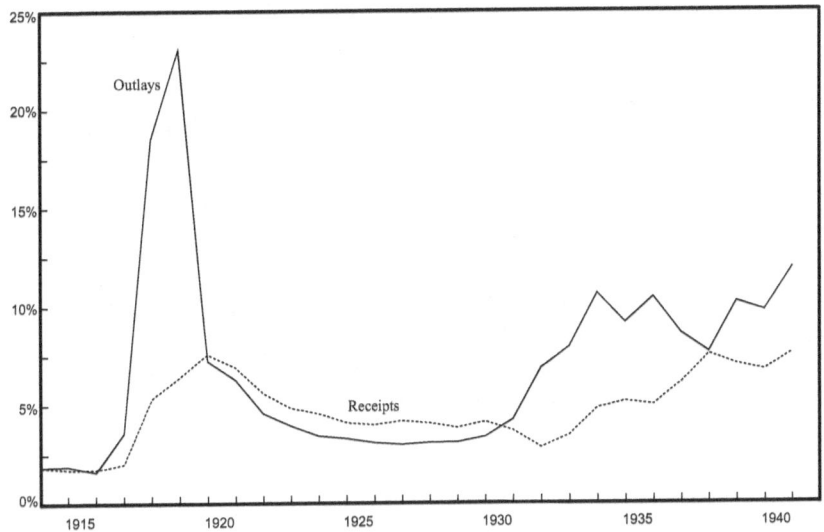

Figure 2.11: U.S. federal government outlays and receipts as percentage of GNP, 1914 - 1941

However, with minimal intervention by the Harding administration (at least by today's standards) and significant cuts in federal government spending (Figures 2.9 to 2.11), the economy improved rapidly in 1922 and 1923. Unemployment fell to 2.4% by 1923 [41, pp. 32, 49-50], [254, p. xxix].

2.4   German Hyperinflation

The postwar experience in many other nations was far worse, particularly in Germany. The Weimar Republic saw no great benefit in maintaining the value of its currency and thus allowed its value to drop precipitously (Figure 2.12). The collapse of the German mark was helpful to state-favored industries that had incurred large debts during the war, as those debts were effectively eliminated. Unlike in the United States, creditors of German war debts were "stiffed" and debtors were bailed out by Germany's monetary policy. The savings of the middle class and workers, however, were wiped out [256, pp. 61-62]. Also, the collapse of the mark did not reduce Germany's reparations burden, as reparation payments were defined in terms of gold.

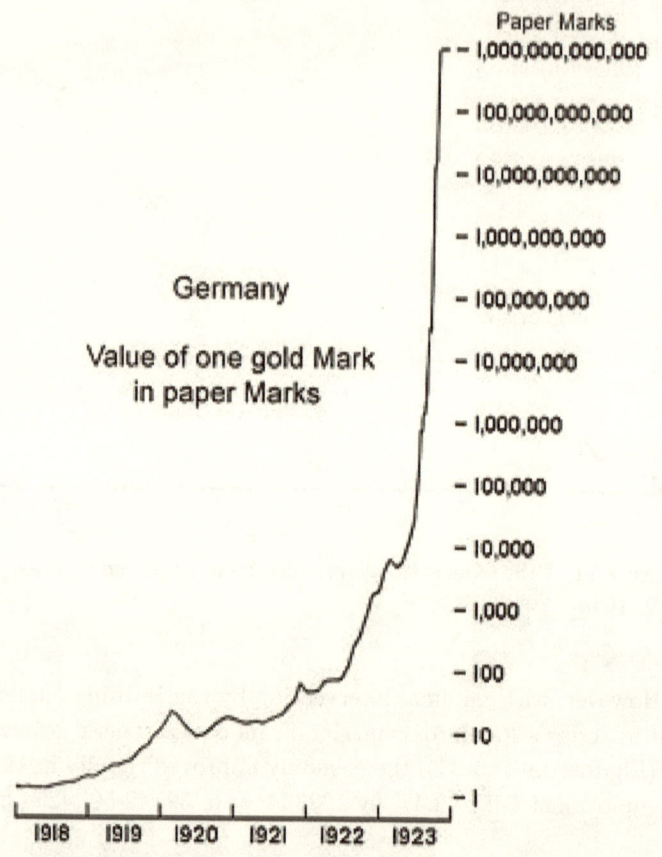

Figure 2.12: Collapse of the German mark after World War I [26]

The hyperinflation in Germany was, in part, a consequence of the necessary postwar economic adjustments as well as the enormous reparations burden. France invaded the industrial Ruhr valley in January 1923 in response to insufficient reparation payments, aggravating the situation [256, p. 61]. Austria, Hungary, and Poland also experienced hyperinflation after the war [1, pp. 16,156,223].

Initially, the depreciation of the currency allowed Germany's unemployment rate to remain low, at 2.8% for 1921 and 1.5% for 1922. As with any inflation, however, a subsequent depression can not be indefinitely avoided. Unemployment rose sharply as the mark completely collapsed, reaching

9.6% in 1923 and 13.5% in 1924 [39].

The Rentenmark was introduced in November 1923. Backed by a mortgage on land and, more importantly, limited in supply, it provided a new stable currency that ended the hyperinflation and created a base for recovery. One Rentenmark equaled 1 trillion of the old paper marks [1, p. 132].

Chapter 3

1923-1929: Imbalances Developing Amid Prosperity

In the 1920s, economic growth spread through America and much of Europe. The decade became known as the "Roaring Twenties" in the United States as the standard of living improved dramatically. Europe also saw economic improvement, including Germany, which had been ravaged by inflation. Unfortunately, some of that growth was built on credit and inflated currencies.

3.1 The Roaring Twenties in the United States

Economic growth in the United States was particularly robust. With the important exception of high tariffs, federal government policies generally encouraged commerce. GNP grew at an average annual rate of 5.2% in current prices and 6.0% in constant prices from 1921 to 1929 (Figure 2.7). A bull market in stocks dominated most of the decade (Figure 3.1). Significant tax cuts (Figure 3.2) and limited government spending helped foster the growth [41, pp. 50, 81-89]. Treasury Secretary Andrew W. Mellon, who served from 1921 to 1932 under three Presidents, is widely recognized as the principal architect of the tax cuts [41, pp. 81-89], [30, pp. 52-53].

The significant productivity improvements of the decade led to impres-

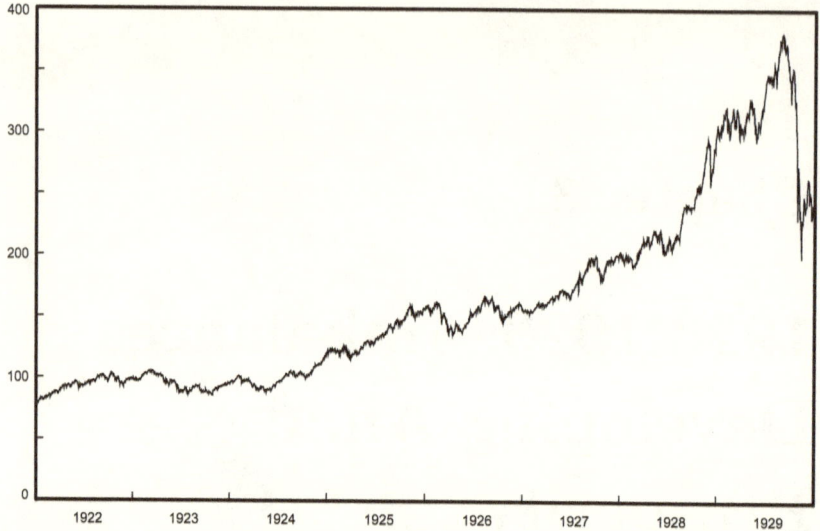

Figure 3.1: Dow Jones Industrial Average, 1922 - 1929 [16]

sive improvements in the standard of living for most Americans. Ownership of private automobiles expanded rapidly. Rural electrification was quickly followed by the introduction of many new electrical appliances into the typical home [41, p. 83-84]. New machines came into use in many areas, such as agriculture and construction, boosting productivity [47,54].

3.2   European Growth

Although generally not as strong as in the United States, economic growth also returned to European nations in the 1920s. Growth rates in western and northern European nations ranged from 2.7% in Great Britain to a strong 6.1% in France (Table 3.1).

The Dawes Plan of 1924 eased Franco-German tensions by setting an interim reparations payment schedule of 1-1.7 billion gold marks per year for four years (with 2.5 billion marks per year scheduled thereafter) [43], and the Young Plan of 1929 permanently fixed the reparations amount at a present value of 37 billion marks, with payments scheduled at an average of 2.05 billion marks per year for 37 years followed by 1.7 billion marks per

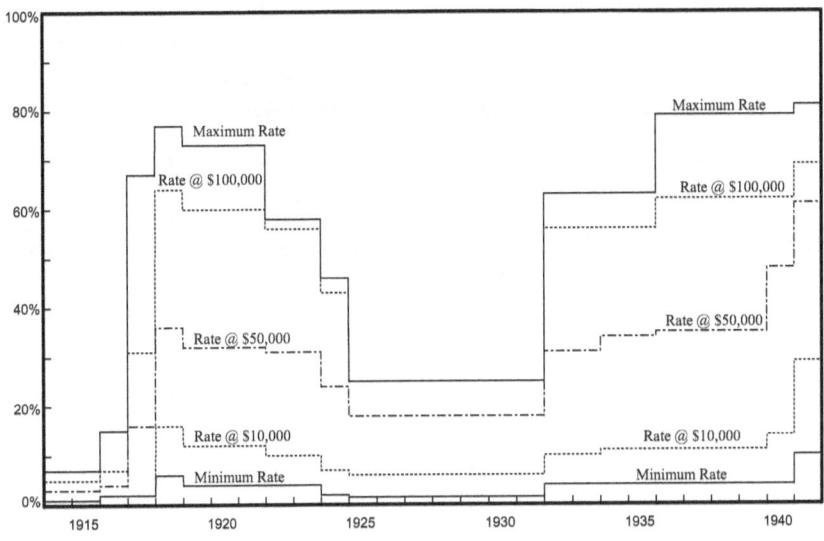

Figure 3.2: U.S. marginal income tax rates, 1914 - 1941 [259]

Nation	Average Growth Rate (constant prices)
Austria (GNP)	4.6%
Czechoslovakia (GDP)	5.7%
Denmark (GDP)	4.6%
Finland (GDP)	5.7%
France (GDP)	6.1%
Great Britain (GDP)	2.7%
Italy (GNP)	3.8%
Norway (GDP)	4.8%
Spain (NNP)	3.4%
Sweden (GDP)	5.0%

Table 3.1: Average annual economic growth in Europe, 1921 - 1929 [39]

year for the following 21 years. 660,000,000 marks of each annual payment was designated as "unconditional," with the remainder being postponable under certain conditions [50].

With a partial relief of reparations burdens, Germany began to attract foreign investment, and the economy began a remarkable but tenuous recovery. U.S. investors loaned Germany $7,000,000,000 during this time despite a substantial risk of default [256, p. 117].

3.3   Tariffs, Protectionism, and a Worldwide Trade War

This growth took place amid an atmosphere of underlying distrust between nations. The United States sought isolationism from European entanglements. European nations sought self-sufficiency in anticipation of a possible future war. The hostile attitudes of World War I had not completely dissipated [5, p. 101, 190-191].

The United States passed the Fordney-McCumber Tariff in September 1922. This protective tariff act more than doubled tariffs on many products. The average tariff rate on imports increased from 15.2% to 36.3% [23]. With this act, U.S. tariffs were the highest in the world outside of Spain [5, p. 61]. These high tariffs blocked debtor nations from selling their goods in the U.S., limiting their ability to pay their dollar debts. Other nations also imposed high tariffs and trade restrictions, reducing the market for U.S. exports [6].

3.4   Growth of Socialism and Statism

The 1910s and 1920s were a time of ascendency of socialist[1] and statist[2] ideas. Communism was on the rise following the 1917 Bolshevik Revolution in Russia. Communists were continually threatening to seize power in Germany from the moment that the Kaiser abdicated the throne on November 9, 1918 [256, pp. 52-55]. The Fascist Party, led by Benito Mussolini, took

---

[1]socialism (n.) - "any of various economic and political theories advocating collective or governmental ownership and administration of the means of production and distribution of goods" [38]

[2]statism (n.) - "concentration of economic controls and planning in the hands of a highly centralized government" [38]

power in Italy in 1922 [25, pp. 48-50]. Great Britain began a "most expensive experiment in socialism" after World War I [186]. Even in the United States, socialist political candidates such as Eugene V. Debs received significant support. Socialist ideas and central planning were also becoming fashionable in intellectual circles as well [257, pp. 182-185].

The rise of socialist ideas in combination with a large scale war meant that government control of many aspects of the economy increased greatly during and after World War I. High tax rates were instituted during the war and maintained even after the war had ended [32, pp. 167-171]. (Even with the Mellon tax cuts, income tax rates and government spending were considerably higher in the United States during the 1920s than they were before the war.) Various forms of industry cartels were formed, with government sanction. Government programs intended to aid the poor and needy also increased. Unemployment insurance was popular in many countries, including Britain [253, pp. 83-84], Germany [144], and Austria [36]. The goals of such government programs were certainly worthy, but they added large new burdens to the economic systems. British trade unions, for example, had less reason to fear layoffs in contract negotiations and thus refused to accept lower wages [253, pp. 83-84]. Economic stresses increased as wage inflexibility hampered necessary adjustments.

3.5 Monetary Inflation Without Rising Prices

Throughout the 1920s, the United States promoted credit expansion and thus inflated the money supply, as demonstrated by Rothbard [254, pp. 85-142]. Although the United States remained on a gold standard, the number of dollars was able to increase due to Federal Reserve management of the fractional reserve banking system (Figure 3.3). The increase in dollars was well in excess of the increase in the nation's gold stock on both an absolute dollar and a percentage basis [253, pp. 24-25] (Figures 3.4 and 3.5). This inflation meant that the potential outstanding claims on the gold supply grew in relation to the gold supply itself. While this situation doesn't cause visible problems during times of economic growth (when increases in production are more than sufficient to pay the claims), it sets the stage for a potential disaster when production inevitably falls behind consumption at some point and holders of dollars discover that there are insufficient goods to back them.

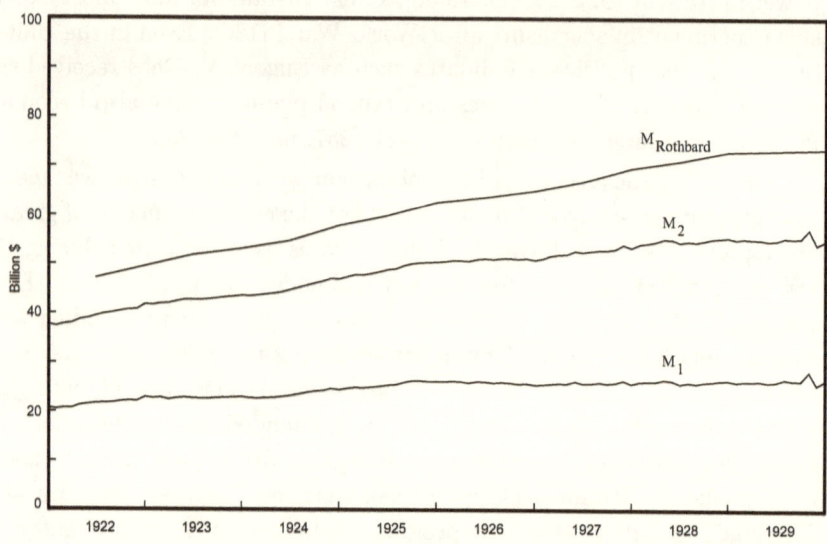

Figure 3.3: United States money supply, 1922 - 1929 [254, p. 92], [21]

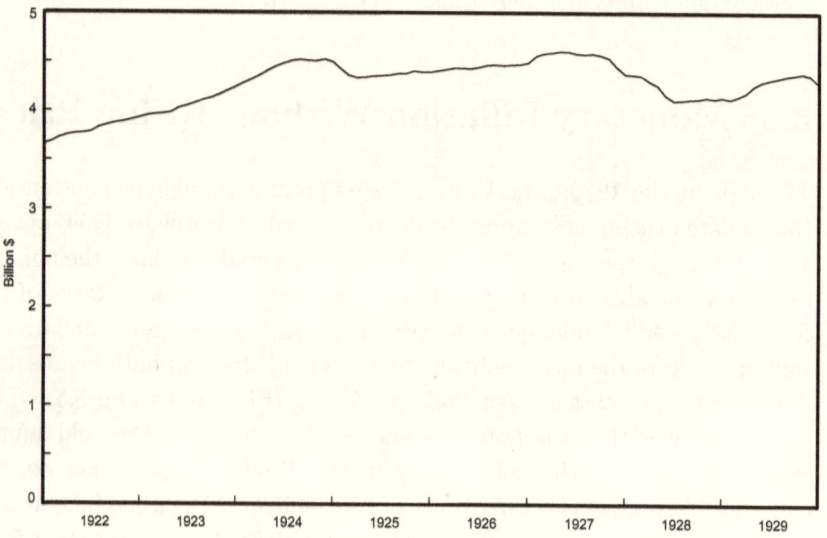

Figure 3.4: United States monetary gold stock, 1922 - 1929, including gold coin in circulation [12]

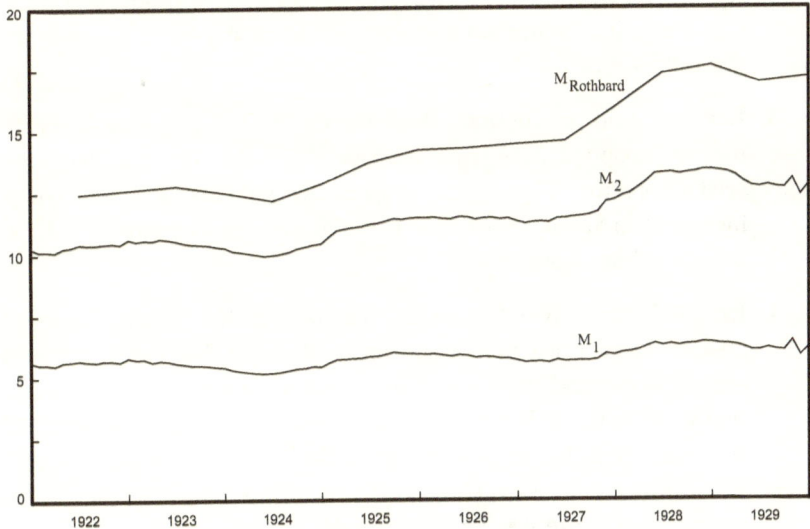

Figure 3.5: Ratio of money supply to monetary gold stock, 1922 - 1929

3.5.1 Price Stabilization

One of the primary objectives of the Federal Reserve was to stabilize prices [254, pp. 169-181]. The rationale behind this objective is highly questionable, however, especially when the currency is defined in terms of a particular commodity (gold). Since prices were defined in terms of gold, it would not be reasonable to expect prices to remain constant if gold production is lagging relative to other products.

There were several forces pushing prices down in the 1920s:

1. The trade war. The trade war imposed a strong downward force on prices of export commodities, particularly agricultural products, as foreign demand for these commodities was sharply curtailed. With significant capital devoted to production of goods for export, the imposition of trade barriers was a significant deflationary force on the overall economy [253, p. 67]. Since the U.S. was a net exporter throughout the 1920s and 1930s, the deflationary impact of the trade war was magnified.

2. Productivity improvements. An increase in productivity throughout

the decade meant that goods became cheaper to produce and hence cost less. Such reductions in cost would be expected to push prices down [254, pp. 169-171].

3. Reduced gold production. With the onset of World War I, gold production dropped 32% from 1915 to 1922 and only gradually recovered afterward (Figure 3.6). With less gold being produced, gold increased in value, and hence prices measured in terms of gold were being pushed down.

4. Residual World War I inflation. The outbreak of war in Europe had created large price increases due to demand for war materiel and shortages of goods in the warring nations. These price increases were sustained in the U.S. by a large increase in the gold stock. Even after the sharp deflation of 1920-21, prices in the U.S. were still about 70% above pre-war levels. These prices would be expected to gradually return toward pre-war levels as foreign capital was rebuilt, restoring worldwide production[3] [249, 250]. (The worldwide trade war accelerated the impact of this process on the United States by choking off exports.)

By inflating the money supply to counteract these forces, the Federal Reserve blocked the important signals that these price changes would provide and thus allowed economic imbalances to build to a dangerous extent.

3.5.2   Foreign Loans

One of the objectives of the inflationary policy was to increase lending to Europe [254, pp. 137-142]. The United States government "encouraged" additional lending to Europe throughout the 1920s in order to offset their war debts and allow Europeans to buy American products. (Simply reducing the tariffs, instead of loaning Europe the money to pay them, would have been far more sensible [254, pp. 139-140].) These loans postponed for a time the adverse impact of the war debts and tariffs [5, p. 135], [254, p. 249] and the monetary inflation postponed the destabilizing effects of high debts in a period of falling prices.

---

[3]A distinct economic pattern has been observed following major wars such as the Napoleonic wars, the U.S. Civil War, and World War I. This pattern consisted of a sharp but short post-war depression (1815, 1866, 1920-21), followed by many years of economic expansion ending in the bursting of a speculative bubble (1825, 1873, 1929) and a harsh, protracted depression [249, 250].

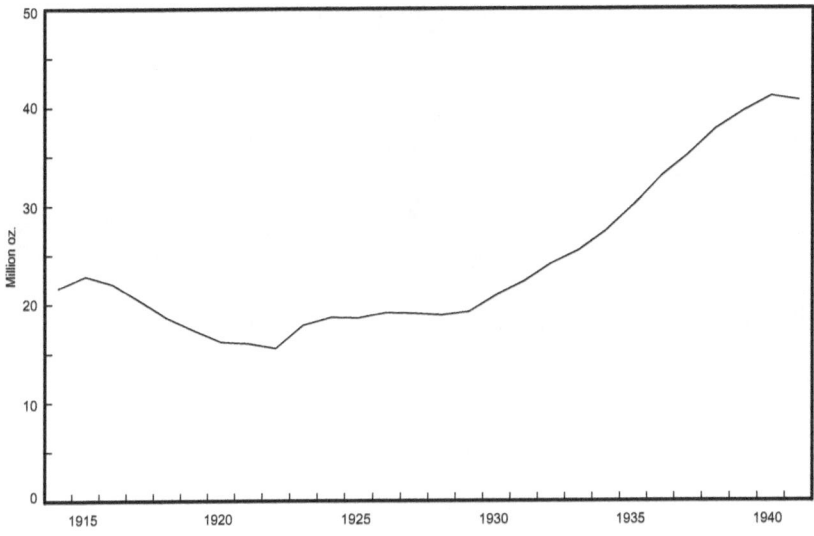

Figure 3.6: Worldwide gold production, 1914 - 1941 [12]

3.6 Gold Exchange Standard

In addition to heavy borrowing, the European nations had inflated their currencies and abandoned the gold standard during World War I. After the war ended, most nations gradually returned to a "gold exchange standard" in an attempt to fix exchange rates again and thus stabilize currency values. Under this standard, a nation's currency was not redeemable for gold directly (unlike a true gold standard), but it was redeemable for British pounds or American dollars at a rate fixed by the central bank of the issuing nation [255, pp. 102-104]. The United States remained on a traditional gold standard. Great Britain returned to a "gold bullion standard" in 1925, by which a fixed number of British pounds was redeemable for a 400-oz. bullion bar [186]. Unlike the U.S., however, the Bank of England did not offer gold coin in exchange for pounds. In comparison to the pre-World War I gold standard, the 1920s monetary systems slowed the movement of gold, allowing bigger monetary and economic imbalances to develop [255, pp. 103-104].

A comparison of the ratio between the money supply and the gold reserves of several nations is shown in Table 3.2. As shown by this table, large

Nation	Dec. 1926	Dec. 1927	Dec. 1928	Dec. 1929	Dec. 1930
Austria	87.9	61.7	35.0	33.4	29.4
France	6.4	5.4	5.1	4.2	3.6
Germany	9.8	11.8	9.5	12.6	13.0
Great Britain	13.1	13.1	13.2	13.2	13.6
Spain	3.7	4.0	4.5	4.7	5.4
Sweden	30.2	30.1	29.6	29.5	31.2
Switzerland	19.5	19.3	20.1	19.7	17.6

Table 3.2: Ratio of money supply (M_2) to gold reserve for selected nations, 1926 - 1930 [12, 39]

differences in these ratios persisted between different nations, even though all of the currencies were defined as weights of gold. These differences were a consequence of several factors. Different banking regulations and reserve requirements in different nations meant that money supply expansion varied from one country to another. The fact that some countries with higher ratios, like the United States, were able to attract gold inflow from other nations with lower ratios reflects confidence in the economies of the higher ratio nations and demand for their currencies. Such confidence developed over a very long period of time. The presence of these differences, however, was a potential source of instability. Confidence acted very much like a dam; if it were to crumble, a flood of gold movements would be unleashed.

Like the pre-World War gold standard, the general expectation was that each nation would expand or contract its money supply to counteract gold inflows or outflows, respectively [5, p. 201]. The system proved, however, to be unstable [255, pp. 102-104].

3.6.1   1925 Resumption of British Gold Standard

On April 28, 1925, Great Britain returned to the gold standard at the pre-war valuation of £3 17s 10½d per troy ounce of fine gold (£1 = \$4.86) [253, pp. 78-80], [32, pp. 30, 39]. Prices in Britain were still too inflated[4] (Figure 3.7), however, for the pound to be properly valued so high, and an increase in union power and other socialist policies prevented wages and

---

[4]In 1925, British prices were 86% above pre-war values, while in the U.S., prices were about 70% above pre-war values.

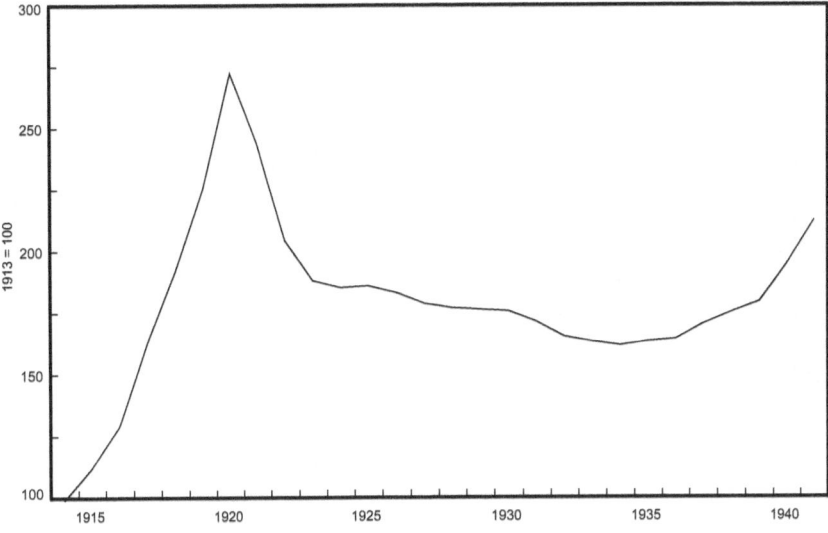

Figure 3.7: British GNP price deflator, 1914 - 1941 [39]

prices from dropping sufficiently to justify such a valuation [6], [254, pp. 142-143]. Hence, with persistent contractionary pressures on the money supply, Britain's economy remained sluggish throughout the remainder of the 1920s with unemployment remaining steadily at or above 7%. The gold bullion standard, however, slowed the outflow of gold (Figure 3.8), allowing the imbalances from the high currency valuation to persist for many years [255, p. 103].

Restoration of the gold standard at a lower parity does not seem to have been considered seriously by the British; to do so would have damaged the country's superb international creditworthiness and been regarded as a blow to Britain's prestige. The classical economist David Ricardo had considered an effort to restore a currency to a previous parity worthwhile if the currency had been devalued by 5%, but he regarded the cost of addressing a 20% devaluation by deflating back to parity as excessive [253, p. 80]. "The 1925 return to the gold standard was perhaps the most decisively damaging action involving money in modern times," according to John Kenneth Galbraith [22, p. 168]. Prices (as measured by the GNP price deflators of Britain and the U.S.) and exchange rates during the 1923-1924 time period [253, p. 80] suggest that the pound was overvalued by 8%-10%;

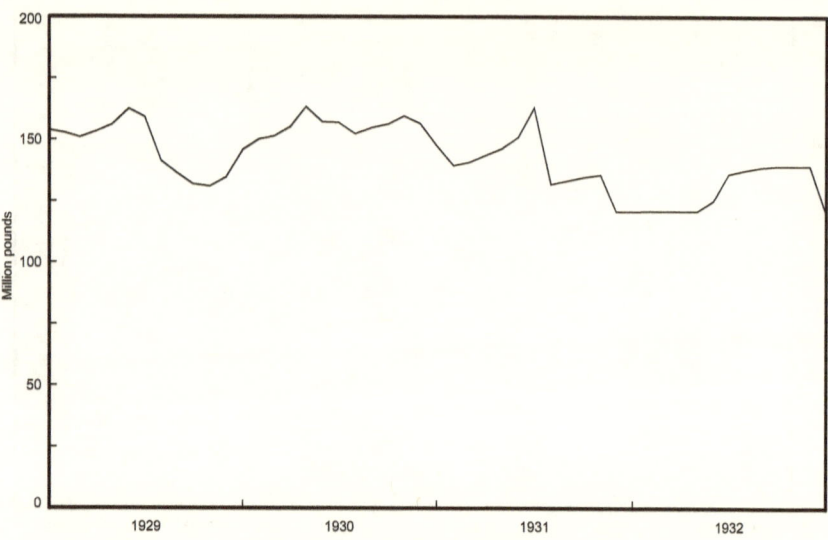

Figure 3.8: British central bank gold reserves, 1929 - 1932 [12]

thus, Galbraith's judgment may have been overly harsh. The U.S., after all, had restored the dollar to gold parity from a 10% devaluation following the Civil War [21, pp. 58-65] by allowing a lengthy period of deflation in the 1870s. As a result of the effort, the U.S. received many long-term benefits – increased foreign and domestic investment and a high credit standing that permitted the borrowing of large amounts of money for many years afterward at low interest rates [5, pp. 210-212]. The discipline required to restore currency parity to gold in both cases was considerable, however.

3.6.2   1928 Resumption of French Gold Standard

Whereas Britain overvalued the pound, France undervalued the franc when it returned to the gold standard in 1928 [253, pp. 9, 25]. The franc was revalued at 58.95 mg of gold (3.92 cents), about one-fifth of its pre-war value [48]. This revaluation actually overstated to some extent the inflation of World War I [253, p. 9, 25], and gold consequently began to steadily stream into France for several years (Figure 3.9). Furthermore, France converted pounds and dollars into gold at most every opportunity [1, p. 145], thus leading to a steady drop in the ratio of francs to gold over several

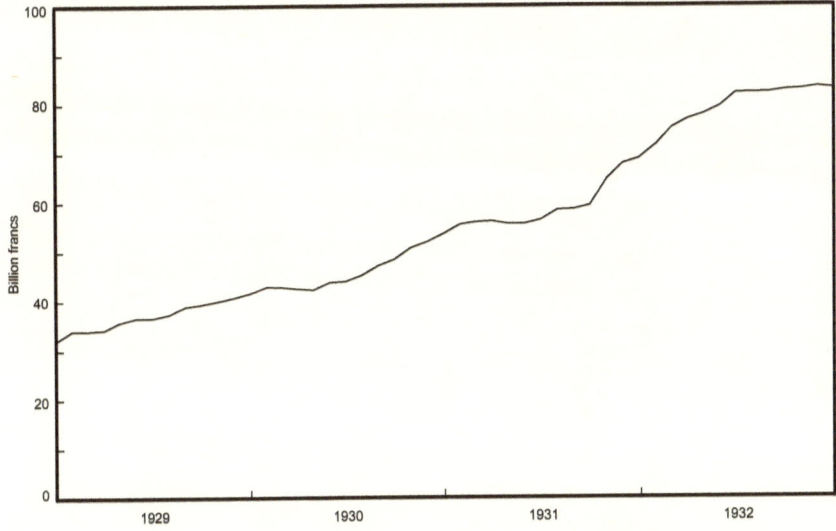

Figure 3.9: French central bank gold reserves, 1929 - 1932 [12]

years.

Chapter 4

1929: The Correction

The magnitude of the economic imbalances that had accumulated during the course of the 1920s was finally revealed in 1929. Booming economic growth that was reaching new heights ended with a resounding crash of the stock market in October, heralding the start of an economic contraction.

The events of the preceding decade made a depression inevitable. It is not at all clear, however, that the events up to this point were sufficient to create a Great Depression of such catastrophic proportions. Had further attempts to defy reality not been tried, the major economic systems might have successfully adjusted and stabilized, albeit at a lower level.

4.1   Stagnation in Europe

As dollar inflation ebbed, loans to Europe dried up, especially as soaring New York stock prices attracted investment money. Interest rates went up in Europe, choking economic growth [5, p. 6]. Germany's economy, which was lacking in capital [253, pp. 8-9, 64], was particularly depressed by the summer of 1929 [5, p. 6]. The Bodenkreditanstalt, a major bank in Austria, became insolvent [254, p. 257].

4.2   U.S. Economy at a Peak

U.S. production reached a peak during the summer. Steel production pushed 100% of capacity (Figure 4.1), and railroad car loadings exceeded

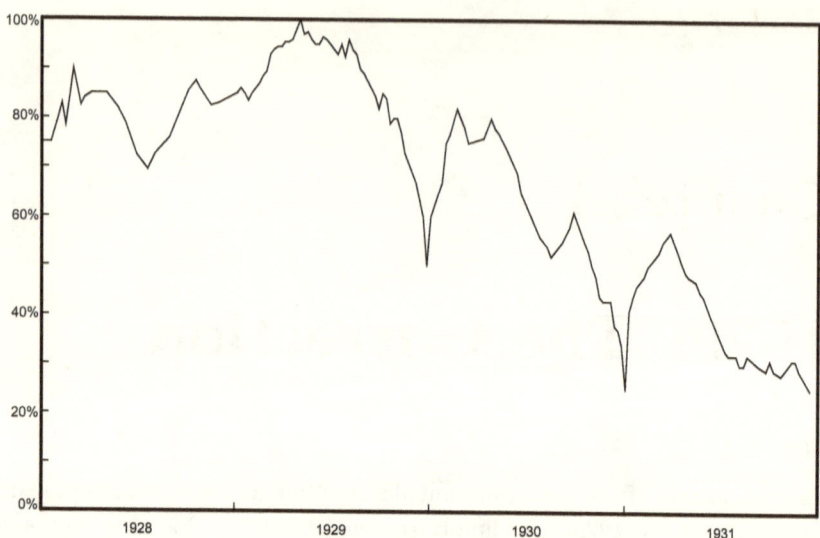

Figure 4.1: Steel production as percentage of capacity, 1928 - 1931 [244]

1,000,000 per week (Figure 4.2). Steel, a market bellwether, was used by
three major sectors of the economy: automobiles, new construction, and
railroads [217]. An early sign of trouble was a large increase in automo-
bile inventories. However, almost all other goods showed no worrisome
inventory levels, and optimism continued to drive stock prices higher into
September [5, pp. 10-17] (Table 4.1). Corporate bond yields were around
5% (Table 4.2). Wheat prices, after falling below $1/bushel on May 27 [49] –
a traditional bear market signal on Wall Street [5, pp. 67-68] – rose sharply
in July to $1.48¼/bushel due to drought in parts of America, Canada,
Argentina, and Australia [51–53], sustaining the optimistic business mood.

The New York Federal Reserve Bank, concerned about the evident bubble in the stock market, opted to raise the discount rate to 6% in August
(Figure 2.5). By restraining credit, this action helped to trigger the subsequent stock market crash and depression [6], [21, pp. 289-291]. (The real
causes of the depression had been building for years, as with most any
depression.)

Tuesday, September 3, 1929			
Company	Stock Price	Annual Dividend Rate	Dividend Yield
Agricultural Equipment			
Case (J.I.) & Co.	350	6	1.7%
International Harvester	140	2.50	1.8%
Autos			
Auburn Auto	497	4 +8% stk	0.8%
General Motors	71³/₄	3.30†	4.6%
Foods			
Coca-Cola	152¹/₂	4	2.6%
General Foods	71⁷/₈	3	4.2%
Hershey Chocolate	124¹/₂	0	0.0%
National Biscuit	212	6.50†	3.1%
Mining			
Anaconda Copper	130⁷/₈	7	5.3%
Colorado Fuel & Iron	66	0	0.0%
Kennecott Copper	92¹/₂	5	5.4%
Railroads			
New York Central	253	8	3.2%
Pennsylvania R.R.	109	4	3.7%
Southern Pacific	156³/₄	6	3.8%
Southern Railway	155¹/₂	8	5.1%
Union Pacific	295	10	3.4%
Retail			
Safeway Stores	181⁵/₈	3	1.7%
Sears Roebuck	171	2.50 +4% stk	1.5%
Woolworth	99	2.40	2.4%
Steel			
Bethlehem Steel	136³/₄	6	4.4%
U.S. Steel	257⁵/₈	7	2.7%
Utilities			
Public Service, N. J.	127⁵/₈	2.60	2.0%
Southern Cal. Edison	86	2	2.3%
Other Industries			
American Tobacco, B	201	8	4.0%
General Electric	391	6†	1.5%
Radio Corporation	98¹/₈	0	0.0%
Standard Oil of N. J.	70³/₄	2†	2.8%
United Aircraft & Tr	134¹/₄	0	0.0%
† – includes extra dividend			

Table 4.1: Selected stock prices at market close, September 3, 1929 [55]

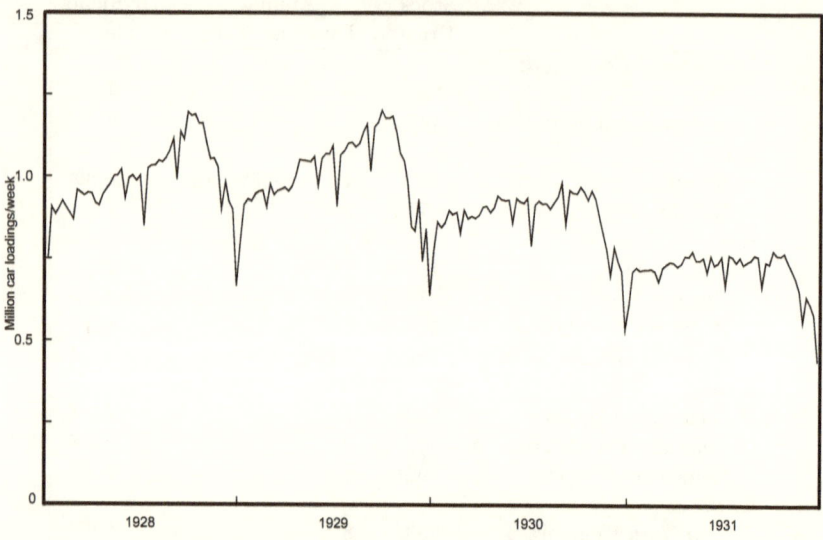

Figure 4.2: Railroad car loadings, 1928 - 1931 [247]

TUESDAY, SEPTEMBER 3, 1929			
Company/Issue	Bond Price	Current Yield	Yield to Maturity
Railroads			
New York Central 5s2013	$103^1/_4$	4.8%	4.8%
Southern Pacific $4^1/_2$s1968	$92^3/_4$	4.9%	4.9%
Southern Railway 4s1956	$85^1/_4$	4.7%	5.0%
Union Pacific 4s1968	$84^1/_4$	4.7%	4.9%
Other Industries			
Bethlehem Steel 5s1936	$100^3/_4$	5.0%	4.9%
General Motors 6s1937	$101^1/_4$	5.9%	5.8%
Standard Oil of N.J. 5s1946	$100^3/_4$	5.0%	4.9%

Table 4.2: Selected bond prices at market close, September 3, 1929 [56]

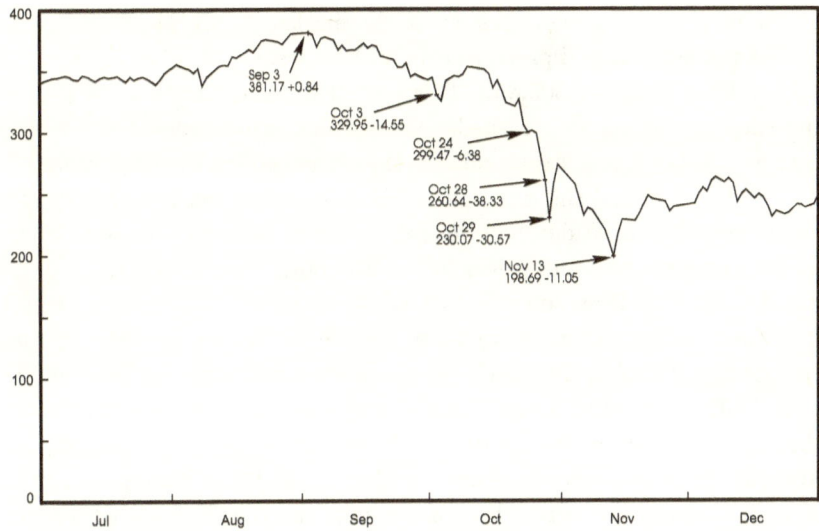

Figure 4.3: Dow Jones Industrial Average, July - December 1929 [16]

4.3   The Stock Market Crash

The value of stock is derived from its ownership of future earnings of a corporation [7], [33, pp. 5-12]. Consequently, stock prices are a "leading indicator" of economic developments, as collectively valuated by the market's participants. However, stock prices, like any price, can occasionally fail to objectively account properly for all relevant economic factors, since the buyers and sellers are human and may not themselves fully recognize all of these factors. In such cases, the markets will rapidly and dramatically readjust toward the equilibrium (usually downward) when enough participants realize the situation, starting a price movement to which others then respond [7].

This situation had developed in United States stock markets by the fall of 1929. By early September, a growing list of poor economic indicators was observable (particularly on the international front), yet stock prices pushed to new highs. The Dow Jones Industrial Average (DJIA) declined quite steadily throughout September, falling 10% from its September 3 closing high of 381.17 (Figure 4.3). A sharp drop of 4% on October 3 was quickly followed by a recovery. After reaching 352.86 on October 10, however, the

DJIA slid 7.5% in less than two weeks, reaching 326.51 on October 22 and driving many small speculators out of the market [5, pp. 24-28], [58].

The market dropped precipitously on Wednesday, October 23, with the DJIA falling 20.66 to 305.85. Then, on Thursday, October 24 ("Black Thursday"), the market crashed. Many stock prices were down 10% or more at midday, but a strong rally in the afternoon cut losses significantly, and the DJIA closed the day down only 6.38 points, at 299.47 [57]. The market steadied on Friday and Saturday, but on Monday, October 28, the market again crashed and prices fell continuously throughout the day [58] (Table 4.3). The Dow Jones Industrial Average fell 38.33 points (12.8%) to 260.64, the largest single-day point decline in the average prior to 1986. On Tuesday, October 29, stock prices crashed again as the Dow fell another 30.57 points (11.7%) on 16,410,030 shares of trading [60] (Table 4.4). The market rallied on Wednesday, with the Dow rising 28.40 (12.3%), but subsequently fell further, dropping to a low of 198.69 on November 13 (Table 4.5). The market bounced off of this low, and the Dow settled within a range between 230 and 265 for the remainder of the year.

4.4   Argentina

Early signs of monetary strain from the depression appeared in South America. In Argentina, the double whammy of a poor wheat crop in conjunction with falling wheat prices worldwide resulted in a steady outflow of gold throughout 1929 (Figure 4.4). Interest rates on bank loans rose to 8.5-9% as currency in circulation contracted by law to reflect the gold outflow. On December 17, Argentine President Irigoyen abruptly closed the gold conversion office, effectively taking Argentina off the gold standard. The move was criticized by many contemporary bankers as unnecessary; Argentina had received a larger inflow of gold from the U.S. in 1927 and 1928 than was exported to the U.S. in 1929. Not surprisingly, Argentina's credit standing was damaged; an $8,000,000 loan that had been virtually signed was abruptly postponed [63–65].

| MONDAY, OCTOBER 28, 1929 | | | | |
| NYSE Volume: 9,212,800 shares | | | | |
Company	Last	Change	Since 9/3/29	Dividend
Agricultural Equipment				
Case (J.I.) & Co.	201	-24	-42.6%	6
International Harvester	$87^3/_4$	$-13^1/_2$	-37.3%	2.50
Autos				
Auburn Auto	190	-25	-61.8%	4 +8% stk
General Motors	$47^1/_2$	$-6^3/_4$	-33.8%	3.30†
Foods				
Coca-Cola	137	$-7^3/_4$	-10.2%	4
General Foods	$48^1/_8$	$-6^3/_8$	-33.0%	3
Hershey Chocolate	112	$-14^1/_2$	-10.0%	0
National Biscuit	180	$-23^1/_4$	-15.1%	7.50†
Mining				
Anaconda Copper	$93^1/_2$	-9	-28.6%	7
Colorado Fuel & Iron	$40^1/_4$	$-8^1/_4$	-39.0%	0
Kennecott Copper	$70^5/_8$	$-6^3/_8$	-23.6%	5
Railroads				
New York Central	186	$-22^5/_8$	-26.5%	8
Pennsylvania R.R.	90	$-6^1/_8$	-17.4%	4
Southern Pacific	128	$-7^1/_2$	-18.3%	6
Southern Railway	142	-4	-8.7%	8
Union Pacific	240	-16	-18.6%	10
Retail				
Safeway Stores	$138^1/_4$	$-9^3/_4$	-23.9%	3
Sears Roebuck	$111^1/_4$	-16	-34.9%	2.50 +4% stk
Woolworth	80	-7	-19.2%	2.40
Steel				
Bethlehem Steel	$94^1/_8$	$-9^3/_8$	-31.2%	6
U.S. Steel	186	$-17^1/_2$	-27.8%	7
Utilities				
Public Service, N. J.	$87^1/_2$	$-9^5/_8$	-31.4%	2.60
Southern Cal. Edison	$59^1/_2$	-9	-30.8%	2
Other Industries				
American Tobacco, B	$195^1/_4$	-21	-2.9%	8
General Electric	250	$-47^1/_2$	-36.1%	6†
Radio Corporation	$40^1/_4$	$-18^3/_8$	-59.0%	0
Standard Oil of N. J.	$64^3/_4$	-8	-8.5%	2†
United Aircraft & Tr	$60^1/_8$	$-14^1/_8$	-55.2%	0
† – includes extra dividend				

Table 4.3: Selected stock prices at market close, October 28, 1929 [59]

Company	Last	Change	Since 9/3/29	Dividend
TUESDAY, OCTOBER 29, 1929				
NYSE Volume: 16,410,030 shares				
Agricultural Equipment				
Case (J.I.) & Co.	201	–	−42.6%	6
International Harvester	80	−7³/₄	−42.9%	2.50
Autos				
Auburn Auto	130	−60	−73.8%	4　　+8% stk
General Motors	40	−7¹/₂	−44.3%	3.30†
Foods				
Coca-Cola	128³/₈	−8⁵/₈	−15.8%	4
General Foods	40	−8¹/₈	−44.3%	3
Hershey Chocolate	86	−26	−30.9%	0
National Biscuit	165	−15	−22.2%	7.50†
Mining				
Anaconda Copper	85	−8¹/₂	−35.1%	7
Colorado Fuel & Iron	35¹/₄	−5	−46.6%	0
Kennecott Copper	65³/₄	−4⁷/₈	−28.9%	5
Railroads				
New York Central	189¹/₂	+3¹/₂	−25.1%	8
Pennsylvania R.R.	82	−8	−24.8%	4
Southern Pacific	124	−4	−20.9%	6
Southern Railway	130	−12	−16.4%	8
Union Pacific	239⁷/₈	− ¹/₈	−18.7%	10
Retail				
Safeway Stores	115	−23¹/₄	−36.7%	3
Sears Roebuck	95	−16¹/₄	−44.4%	2.50 +4% stk
Woolworth	75	−5	−24.2%	2.40
Steel				
Bethlehem Steel	84	−10¹/₈	−38.6%	6
U.S. Steel	174	−12	−32.5%	8†
Utilities				
Public Service, N. J.	73¹/₂	−14	−42.4%	2.60
Southern Cal. Edison	53	−6¹/₂	−38.4%	2
Other Industries				
American Tobacco, B	186	−9¹/₄	−7.5%	8
General Electric	222	−28	−43.2%	6†
Radio Corporation	38¹/₂	−1³/₄	−60.8%	0
Standard Oil of N. J.	57³/₄	−7	−18.4%	2†
United Aircraft & Tr	41	−19¹/₈	−69.5%	0
† – includes extra dividend				

Table 4.4: Selected stock prices at market close, October 29, 1929 [61]

WEDNESDAY, NOVEMBER 13, 1929				
Company	Stock Price	Since 9/3/29	Annual Dividend Rate	Dividend Yield
Agricultural Equipment				
Case (J.I.) & Co.	130	−62.9%	6	4.6%
International Harvester	$65^{7}/_{8}$	−52.9%	2.50	3.8%
Autos				
Auburn Auto	$130^{1}/_{4}$	−73.8%	4 +8% stk	3.1%
General Motors	$36^{1}/_{8}$	−49.7%	3.30†	9.1%
Foods				
Coca-Cola	101	−33.8%	4	4.0%
General Foods	40	−44.3%	3	7.5%
Hershey Chocolate	45	−63.9%	0	0.0%
National Biscuit	140	−34.0%	7.50†	5.4%
Mining				
Anaconda Copper	$70^{1}/_{2}$	−46.1%	7	9.9%
Colorado Fuel & Iron	$28^{3}/_{4}$	−56.4%	0	0.0%
Kennecott Copper	$50^{1}/_{2}$	−45.4%	5	9.9%
Railroads				
New York Central	160	−36.8%	8	5.0%
Pennsylvania R.R.	$75^{1}/_{8}$	−31.1%	4	5.3%
Southern Pacific	106	−32.4%	6	5.7%
Southern Railway	115	−26.0%	8	7.0%
Union Pacific	200	−32.2%	10	5.0%
Retail				
Safeway Stores	94	−48.2%	3	3.2%
Sears Roebuck	$81^{3}/_{8}$	−52.4%	2.50 +4% stk	3.1%
Woolworth	$52^{1}/_{2}$	−47.0%	2.40	4.6%
Steel				
Bethlehem Steel	$79^{1}/_{4}$	−42.0%	6	7.6%
U.S. Steel	$151^{1}/_{2}$	−41.2%	8†	5.3%
Utilities				
Public Service, N. J.	$54^{1}/_{2}$	−57.3%	2.60	4.8%
Southern Cal. Edison	47	−45.3%	2	4.3%
Other Industries				
American Tobacco, B	$172^{1}/_{2}$	−14.2%	10†	5.8%
General Electric	173	−55.8%	6†	3.5%
Radio Corporation	$28^{3}/_{4}$	−70.7%	0	0.0%
Standard Oil of N. J.	$50^{3}/_{4}$	−28.3%	2†	3.9%
United Aircraft & Tr	$31^{1}/_{8}$	−76.8%	0	0.0%
† − includes extra dividend				

Table 4.5: Selected stock prices at market close, November 13, 1929 [62]

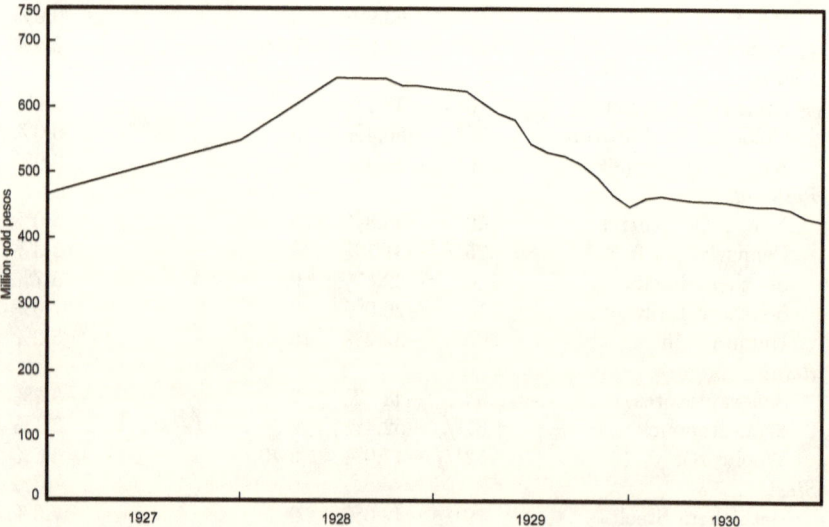

Figure 4.4: Argentina central bank gold reserves, 1927 - 1930 [12]

Chapter 5

1930: Compounding the Situation

Economic output shrank in the last quarter of 1929. However, a vigorous revival occurred in the spring of 1930, as production returned to roughly the levels of 1928 [5, p. 57] (Figures 4.1 and 4.2). Stock prices also rebounded steadily (Table 5.1), with the Dow reaching a post-crash high of 294.07 on April 17 – near its value prior to the Black Monday crash of October 28, 1929. Bond prices rallied as well, reducing yields and borrowing costs (Table 5.2). However, economic activity soon dropped off significantly as international developments continued to worsen, hampering exports. Poor earnings reports led to a resumption of the stock market decline (Figure 5.1), with the DJIA falling sharply in June and sliding to 164.58 at the end of the year (Table 5.4). Bond prices, which had risen as interest rates fell, sagged in the last three months of 1930 as credit risks increased (Table 5.3).

The economic situation was greatly aggravated by many of the government responses to the depression. Unlike previous Presidents, Herbert Hoover sought government intervention in the economy in an attempt to improve the situation. These actions instead made the situation far worse [254, pp. 186-189], [41, pp. 27-62].

Company	Stock Price	Since 9/3/29	Annual Dividend Rate		Dividend Yield
THURSDAY, APRIL 17, 1930					
Agricultural Equipment					
Case (J.I.) & Co.	$319\frac{1}{2}$	−8.7%	6		1.9%
International Harvester	$113\frac{1}{2}$	−18.9%	2.50		2.2%
Autos					
Auburn Auto	258	−48.1%	4	+8% stk	1.6%
General Motors	$51\frac{1}{4}$	−28.6%	3.30†		6.4%
Foods					
Coca-Cola	$183\frac{7}{8}$	+20.6%	6		3.3%
General Foods	$52\frac{3}{4}$	−26.6%	3		5.7%
Hershey Chocolate	$101\frac{3}{4}$	−18.3%	5		4.9%
National Biscuit	88	+3.8%*	2.80		3.2%
Mining					
Anaconda Copper	$69\frac{7}{8}$	−46.6%	7		10.0%
Colorado Fuel & Iron	$71\frac{3}{4}$	+8.7%	2		2.8%
Kennecott Copper	$52\frac{7}{8}$	−42.8%	5		9.5%
Railroads					
New York Central	$181\frac{3}{4}$	−28.2%	8		4.4%
Pennsylvania R.R.	$82\frac{3}{8}$	−24.4%	4		4.9%
Southern Pacific	$124\frac{3}{4}$	−20.4%	6		4.8%
Southern Railway	119	−23.5%	8		6.7%
Union Pacific	232	−21.4%	10		4.3%
Retail					
Safeway Stores	$99\frac{1}{4}$	−45.4%	5		5.0%
Sears Roebuck	$92\frac{3}{8}$	−46.0%	2.50	+4% stk	2.7%
Woolworth	$65\frac{1}{2}$	−33.8%	2.40		3.7%
Steel					
Bethlehem Steel	105	−23.2%	6		5.7%
U.S. Steel	$195\frac{1}{4}$	−24.2%	7		3.6%
Utilities					
Public Service, N. J.	117	−8.3%	3.40		2.9%
Southern Cal. Edison	70	−18.6%	2		2.9%
Other Industries					
American Tobacco, B	245	+21.9%	8		3.3%
General Electric	93	−4.9%*	1.60		1.7%
Radio Corporation	$62\frac{3}{8}$	−36.4%	0		0.0%
Standard Oil of N. J.	$78\frac{1}{2}$	+11.0%	2†		2.5%
United Aircraft & Tr	$91\frac{1}{2}$	−31.8%	0		0.0%
† – includes extra dividend			* – reflects stock split		

Table 5.1: Selected stock prices at market close, April 17, 1930 [68]

Figure 5.1: Dow Jones Industrial Average, 1930 [16]

THURSDAY, APRIL 10, 1930			
Company/Issue	Bond Price	Current Yield	Yield to Maturity
Railroads			
New York Central 5s2013	$107^1/_2$	4.7%	4.6%
Pennsylvania R.R. $4^1/_2$s1970	$94^3/_4$	4.7%	4.8%
Southern Pacific $4^1/_2$s1968	$97^1/_4$	4.6%	4.7%
Southern Railway 4s1956	$90^3/_4$	4.4%	4.6%
Union Pacific 4s1968	$90^1/_8$	4.4%	4.5%
Utilities			
Public Service E&G $4^1/_2$s1970	$97^1/_2$	4.6%	4.6%
Other Industries			
Bethlehem Steel 5s1936	$101^5/_8$	4.9%	4.7%
General Motors 6s1937	$103^1/_4$	5.8%	5.4%
Standard Oil of N.J. 5s1946	$103^3/_8$	4.8%	4.7%

Table 5.2: Selected bond prices at market close, April 10, 1930 [67]

5.1   Smoot-Hawley Tariff

The Smoot-Hawley Tariff, named for its chief sponsors Senator Reed Smoot (R-Utah) and Representative Willis C. Hawley (R-Oregon) [242], was perhaps the most critical government mistake following the 1929 stock market crash. This act substantially increased already high tariffs and created new tariffs on many goods [70,71]. Its passage and signing by President Hoover generated retaliatory tariffs by numerous other nations. Trade walls thus were raised further, promising even more long-term economic decline (Figure 5.2) [5, pp. 63, 71], [41, pp. 42-45], [254, pp. 241-243].

It is quite remarkable that virtually all economists of the time denounced the tariff and urged Hoover to veto it. Their petition bore over 1,000 signatures [69]. The stock market also apparently registered an opinion on Smoot-Hawley by sliding sharply in June as the act neared completion. Hoover's announcement on Sunday, June 15 that he would sign the bill [254, p. 242], [71] was met the next day by a 14.20-point plunge in the DJIA to 230.05 [72]. (For the month, the Dow fell 17.7%.) Some authors also identify its development in Congress during the previous fall as a trigger or even a cause of the 1929 stock market crash [30, pp. 225-226], [32, p. 225]. The tariff act today remains notorious; although there is no way of knowing whether the depression would have been Great had Smoot-Hawley not been passed, it undoubtedly added to one of the fundamental causes of the economic difficulties [6].

5.2   Federal Farm Board subsidies

Hoover sought to establish a federal program for supporting agricultural prices for farmers in 1929. The Agricultural Marketing Act, passed by Congress in June 1929, created the Federal Farm Board and appropriated $500,000,000 for low-interest loans to farm cooperatives and for the purchase of grains to stabilize prices through the formation of stabilization corporations. The Farmers' National Grain Corporation was created by the Farm Board shortly after the 1929 stock market crash with $10,000,000 capital. It soon began to buy wheat in an attempt to stabilize wheat prices. The following spring (1930), Congress appropriated an additional $100,000,000 for the Farm Board, and the Grain Stabilization Corporation replaced the Farmers' National Grain Corporation. The Farm Board also established a Cotton Stabilization Corporation in June 1930 in a parallel

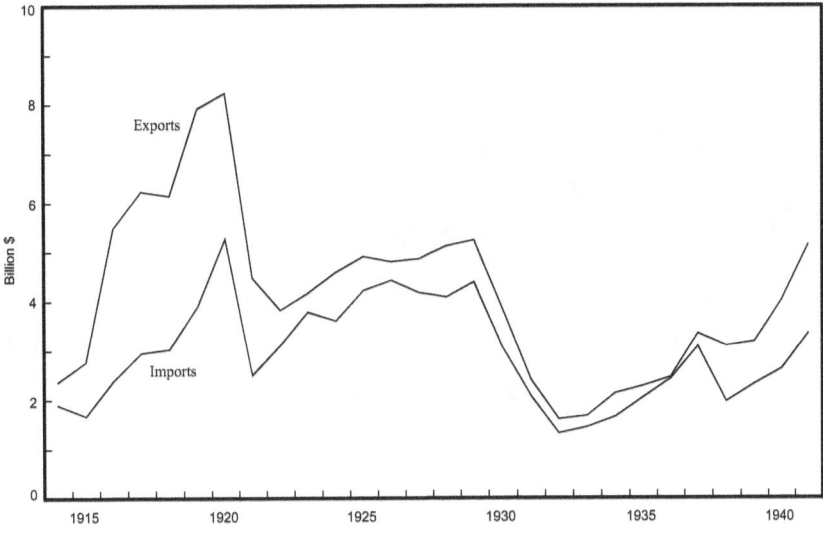

Figure 5.2: U.S. foreign trade, 1914 - 1941 [29]

effort to support cotton prices [254, pp. 227-232].

The Grain Stabilization Corporation accumulated 65,000,000 bushels of wheat by June 30, 1930, yet wheat prices were continuing a steady downward trend. When wheat prices reached $0.73/bushel on the Chicago futures market on November 15, the Grain Stabilization Corporation began to aggressively purchase wheat to establish a price floor at that point for the 1930 crop [254, p. 231], [73]. The purchases included all futures contracts with delivery dates up to and including May 1931. Without any federal government support, the July 1931 wheat contract price broke sharply to $62^{7}/_{8}$¢/bushel by the end of the year [75].

Naturally, since farmers were promised a subsidized price, they continued to grow large crops. Unfortunately, because of the trade war, there was no one to sell them to; Europe had protected, via tariffs, sufficient crop production for their domestic needs [5, p. 48]. The price supports would soon prove unsustainable (Figures 5.3 to 5.6), but not before the creation of truly enormous crop surpluses in 1930 and 1931 [5, pp. 109, 112-113].

Since agriculture employed about 25% of America's work force, the crash of agriculture prices rippled through other sectors of the economy as well [5, p. 70].

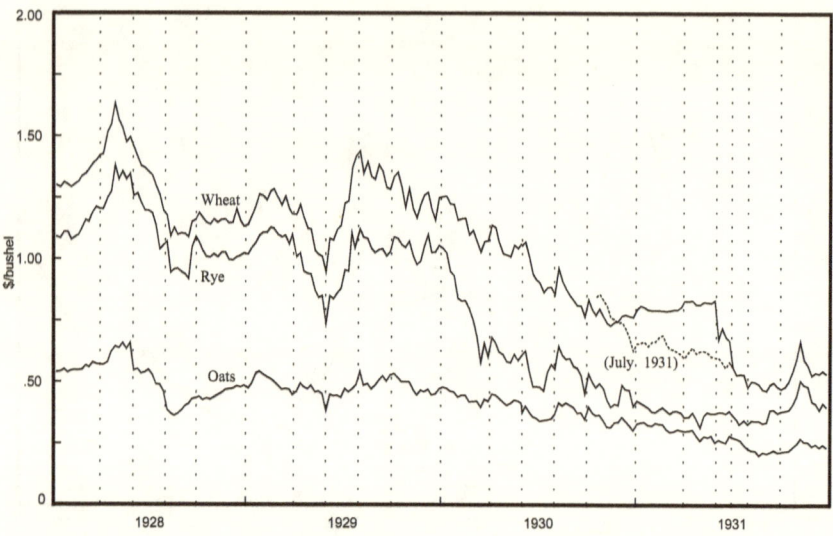

Figure 5.3: Weekly Chicago grain futures prices (continuous front contract price), 1928 - 1931 [245]

5.3 Wage Maintenance

Hoover strongly persuaded business leaders to hold wage levels steady as the depression developed, even though prices were falling. This meant a significant increase in real wages for many workers, but it also, of course, caused unemployment to skyrocket [254, pp. 210-214, 249, 264-270, 285, 321]. Furthermore, many workers who did retain jobs could not have felt very secure about their employment, and hence they undoubtedly saved a considerable portion of their income, awaiting better times for consumption and/or investment.

5.4 Government Spending

Although the term was not in the public lexicon at the time, there was no shortage of government "stimulus" spending in the early 1930s. Hoover advocated large-scale public works projects as a means of employing the unemployed. The idea was certainly understandable from the standpoint of aiding displaced workers without simply subsidizing idleness, but the

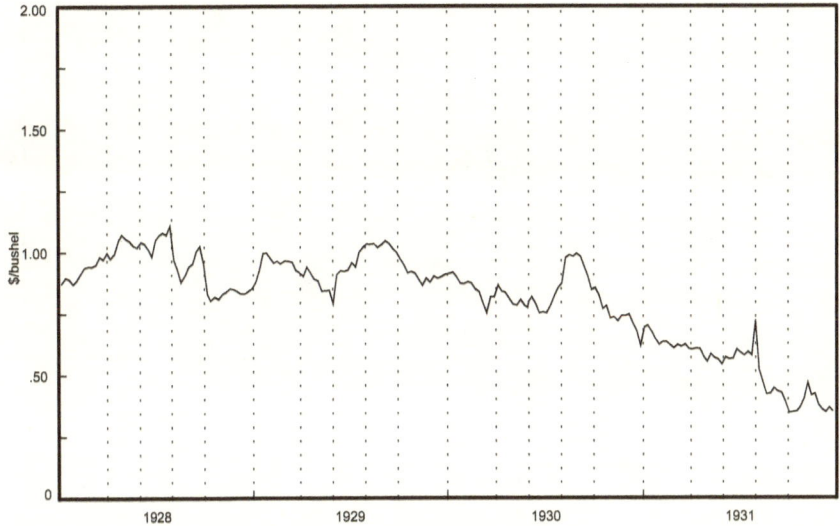

Figure 5.4: Weekly Chicago corn futures prices (continuous front contract price), 1928 - 1931 [245]

economic burden only made the overall situation worse[1] [254, pp. 192-199, 216-217, 250-253, 264-267]. Hoover himself developed serious doubts about the efficacy of public works projects within a couple of years (after seeing the economic catastrophe unfold) [254, p. 295].

There was also growth in the federal bureaucracy, as 26 new commissions were created in the first two years of Hoover's presidency [92].

Prices dropped significantly in 1930, but because federal government nominal spending actually increased 7.7% for fiscal year[2] (FY) 1930-31 over FY 1929-30, government spending rose significantly (16%) in real terms and 25% as a share of GNP (from 3.4% to 4.2%) (Figures 2.9 to 2.11). State

---

[1]One may cite Hoover Dam as an example of economic value created by public works spending. While the project certainly has much value today, its value in the 1930s was considerably less without the high demand for electricity [254, p. 247]. The cost of such projects was in excess of the value they could provide at the time. Also, had these projects been undertaken later, new technology could have reduced the cost of their construction. Advocating such spending is analogous to promoting a federal airport construction program in the 1870s or a program of spaceport construction today.

[2]The federal government fiscal year began on July 1 and ended on June 30 of the following calendar year.

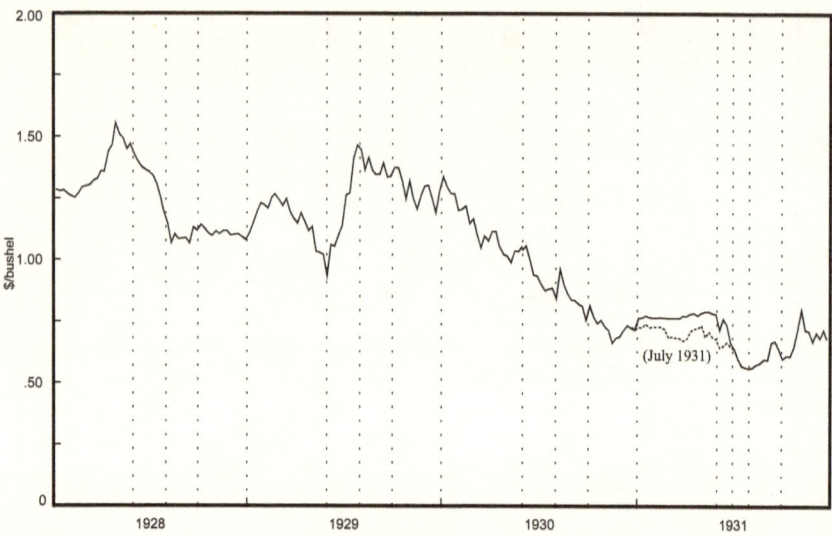

Figure 5.5: Weekly Minneapolis wheat futures prices (continuous front contract price), 1928 - 1931 [245]

and local government spending increases were larger – 8.5% in dollars for calendar year 1930 ($8.9 billion) over calendar year 1929 ($8.2 billion) [254, p. 343]. This increase was 13% after adjusting for price deflation. As a percentage of GNP, state and local government spending (which was a much larger share of overall government spending at the time) increased from 7.8% in 1929 to 9.7% in 1930 (a 14% increase). These increases in government spending competed with private investment and added to the burdens on the economy.

5.5 Easy Money Policy

The Federal Reserve sought to pump more credit into the economy [254, pp. 239-241]. The discount rate was rapidly lowered from 6% to 5% on November 1, 1929 and in $1/2$% increments after that to $2^1/_2$% on June 20, 1930 (Figure 2.5). It was reduced again to 2% on December 24, 1930. However, with many burdens on the economy still in place, the extra credit only served to keep unproductive business and capital afloat and thus inhibited

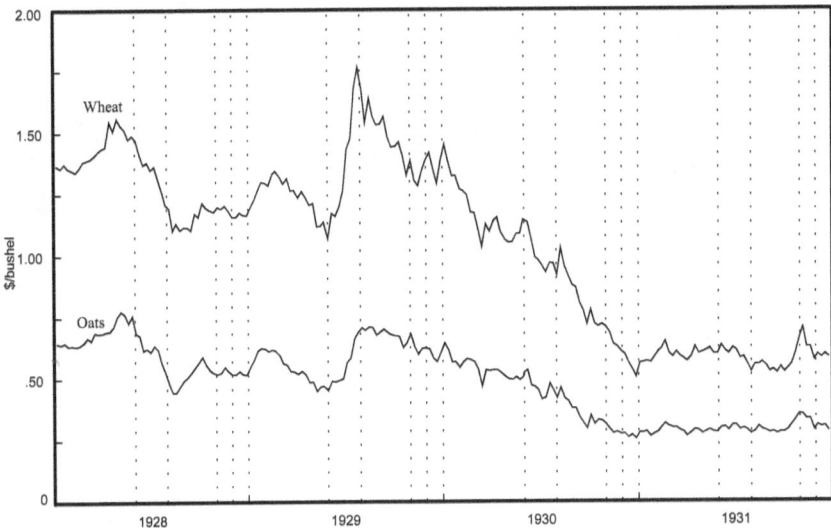

Figure 5.6: Weekly Winnipeg grain futures prices (continuous front contract price), 1928 - 1931 [245]

the liquidation that was needed to restore growth [254, p. 19], [253, pp. 72-75]. It also served to further strain an already shaky banking system.

Whereas favorable business conditions in the 1920s accelerated the growth of the money supply following discount rate cuts, the poor business conditions of 1930 resulted in little demand for new loans, and thus the money supply remained stagnant throughout the year (Figure 5.7). (Nevertheless, with the price decline, the money supply was expanding in real terms, especially in the first half of the year.) Gold streamed into the U.S. steadily throughout 1930 (Figure 5.8) as repayments on foreign loans came in [21, p. 342]. This inflow reduced the ratio of money to gold (Figure 5.9), offsetting some of the earlier inflation. The ratio was still higher than its level during most of 1927.

Secretary Mellon recommended that liquidation be allowed to proceed as needed ("purge the rottenness") to rebalance the economy and restore a foundation for growth [254, p. 210], [41, pp. 28-30]. This advice was economically sound, but it would have meant liquidating a substantial number of industries that produced goods for export and thus would have resulted in a very deep contraction (though probably not as deep as what ultimately

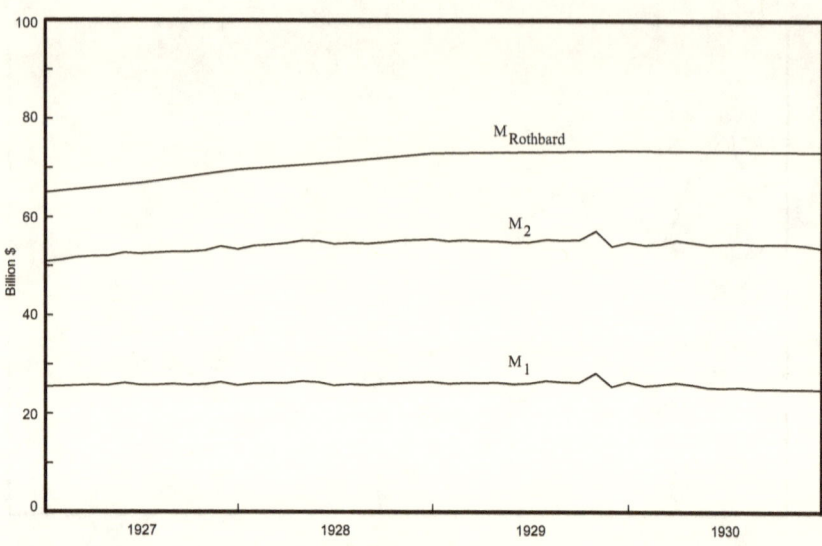

Figure 5.7: United States money supply, 1927 - 1930 [254, pp. 92, 240], [21]

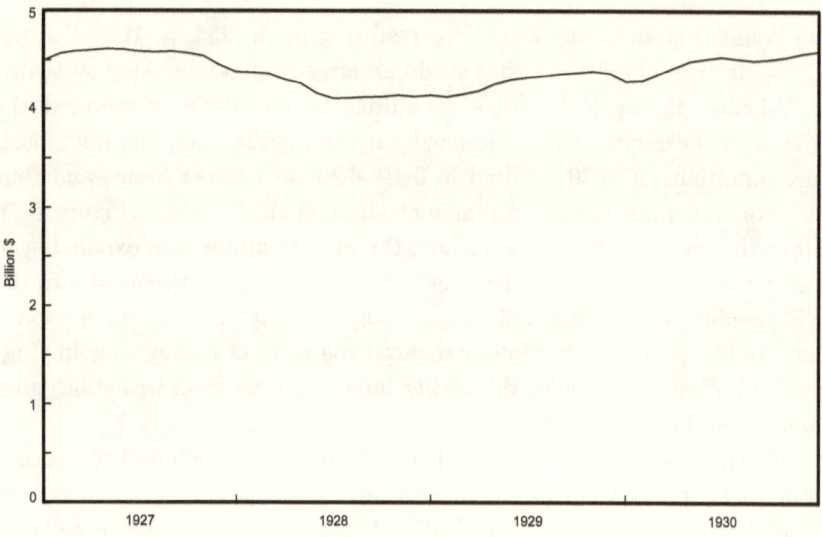

Figure 5.8: United States monetary gold stock, 1927 - 1930, including gold coin in circulation [12]

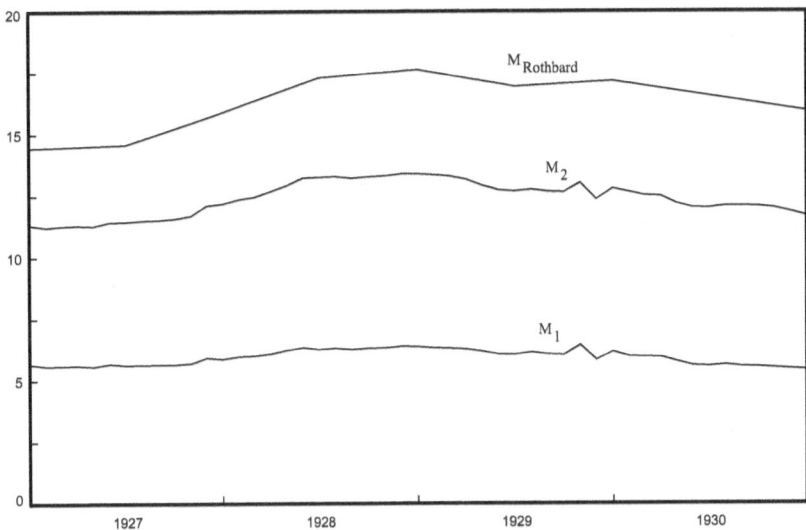

Figure 5.9: Ratio of money supply to monetary gold stock, 1927 - 1930

occurred). The availability of cheap credit allowed many of these industries to hang on for a while, but with scant prospects of improvement in the international trade situation, these industries, and the economy as a whole, were in a state of limbo.

5.6 Bank Runs

By October 1930, the first major wave of the bank runs that would symbolize the depression had begun (Figures 5.10 and 5.11). Most of these runs occurred in rural banks in agricultural states (Missouri, Illinois, Indiana, Iowa, Arkansas, and North Carolina) and were associated with the difficulties in the agricultural sector. They were a consequence of the sharp drop in agricultural prices, which produced a corresponding devaluation in the land which backed the mortgage assets of banks in the Midwest. Because of fractional reserve banking, many banks' assets were exceeded by deposit liabilities, and bank runs resulted [9], [253, p. 120]. For the year, 1,350 banks failed [13, 29].

On December 11, the Bank of United States closed. This bank had

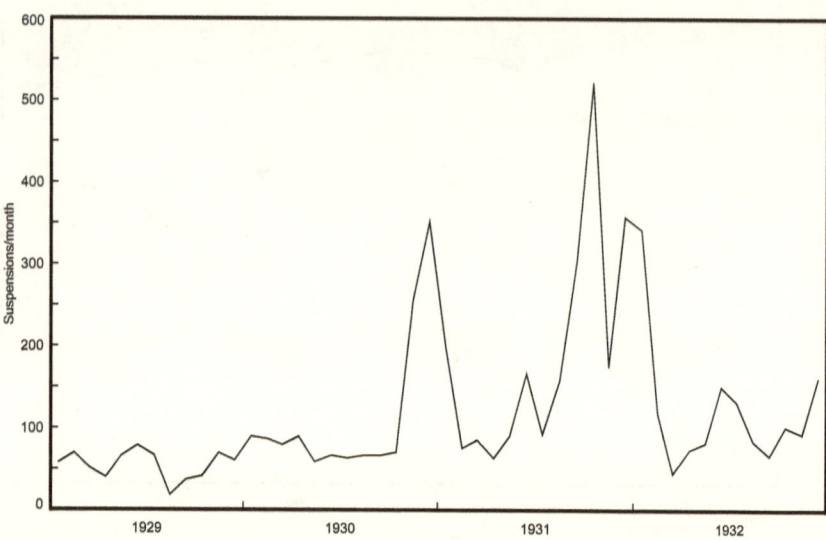

Figure 5.10: Monthly bank suspensions, 1929 - 1932 [13]

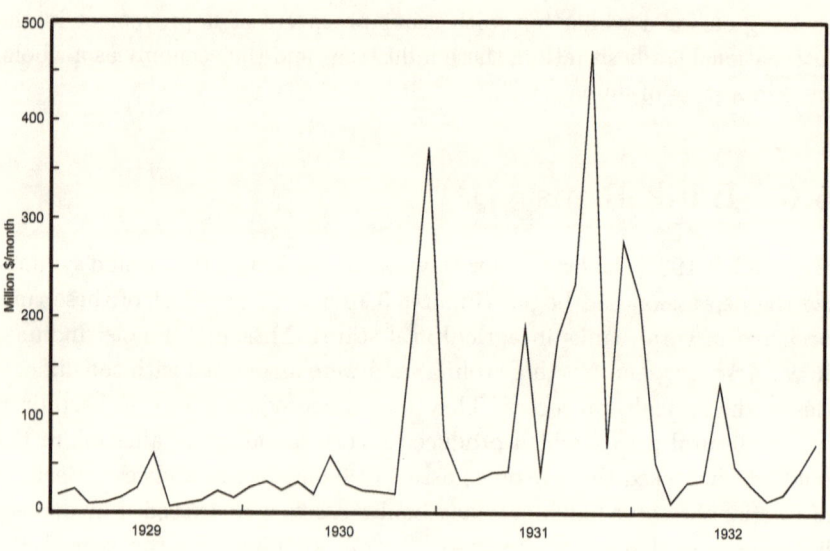

Figure 5.11: Monthly suspended bank deposits, 1929 - 1932 [13]

WEDNESDAY, DECEMBER 17, 1930			
Company/Issue	Bond Price	Current Yield	Yield to Maturity
Railroads			
New York Central 5s2013	105	4.8%	4.8%
Pennsylvania R.R. 4$1/2$s1970	94	4.8%	4.8%
Southern Pacific 4$1/2$s1968	92$7/8$	4.8%	4.9%
Southern Railway 4s1956	82$1/4$	4.9%	5.3%
Union Pacific 4s1968	89$3/4$	4.5%	4.6%
Utilities			
Public Service E&G 4$1/2$s1970	100$1/4$	4.5%	4.5%
Other Industries			
Bethlehem Steel 5s1936	97$1/2$	5.1%	5.5%
General Motors 6s1937	101$3/4$	5.9%	5.7%
Standard Oil of N.J. 5s1946	103	4.9%	4.7%

Table 5.3: Selected bond prices at market close, December 17, 1930 [74]

over $200,000,000 in deposits, and its failure was the largest commercial bank failure up to that time. Unlike most of the bank failures that year, the Bank of United States was situated in New York City, and its failure significantly shook confidence throughout the economy. (It was an ordinary commercial bank, but its name caused some to believe it had some sort of official status.) Like most other bank failures of 1930, however, real estate depreciation was a primary culprit [5, p. 245], [21, pp. 309-311].

The bank runs up to this point, however, did not (yet) constitute a nationwide loss of confidence in the banking system or the currency. Bank failures and suspensions were common even during the boom years of the 1920s, with an average of over 630 per year. The failure of the Bank of United States was regarded by many as the consequence of dubious business practices [9]. Retail sales for 1930 were down from 1929, but not sharply [5, p. 89]. Bonds rallied sharply in the last two weeks of the year (Table 5.5). The international business depression was clearly getting severe, but it was not yet Great.

WEDNESDAY, DECEMBER 31, 1930			
Company	Stock Price	Annual Dividend Rate	Dividend Yield
Agricultural Equipment			
Case (J.I.) & Co.	$89^3/_8$	6	6.7%
International Harvester	50	2.50	5.0%
Autos			
Auburn Auto	$106^1/_4$	4 +8% stk	3.8%
General Motors	$35^3/_8$	3.30†	9.3%
Foods			
Coca-Cola	146	6	4.1%
General Foods	49	3	6.1%
Hershey Chocolate	88	5	5.7%
National Biscuit	$77^5/_8$	3.30†	4.3%
Mining			
Anaconda Copper	30	2.50	8.3%
Colorado Fuel & Iron	$21^1/_2$	1	4.7%
Kennecott Copper	$23^1/_4$	2	8.6%
Railroads			
New York Central	$114^1/_2$	8	7.0%
Pennsylvania R.R.	$56^1/_4$	4	7.1%
Southern Pacific	$93^3/_4$	6	6.4%
Southern Railway	$50^3/_4$	8	15.8%
Union Pacific	180	10	5.6%
Retail			
Safeway Stores	$40^7/_8$	5	12.2%
Sears Roebuck	$45^1/_8$	2.50 +4% stk	5.5%
Woolworth	$55^1/_2$	2.40	4.3%
Steel			
Bethlehem Steel	$50^1/_2$	6	11.9%
U.S. Steel	$139^1/_8$	7	5.0%
Utilities			
Public Service, N. J.	$74^1/_2$	3.40	4.6%
Southern Cal. Edison	46	2	4.3%
Other Industries			
American Tobacco, B	$106^1/_8$	5	4.7%
General Electric	$43^5/_8$	1.60	3.7%
Radio Corporation	12	0	0.0%
Standard Oil of N. J.	$47^1/_8$	2†	4.2%
United Aircraft & Tr	24	0	0.0%
† – includes extra dividend			

Table 5.4: Selected stock prices at market close, December 31, 1930 [76]

WEDNESDAY, DECEMBER 31, 1930			
Company/Issue	Bond Price	Current Yield	Yield to Maturity
Railroads			
New York Central 5s2013	107	4.7%	4.7%
Pennsylvania R.R. 4$^1/_2$s1970	97$^1/_8$	4.6%	4.7%
Southern Pacific 4$^1/_2$s1968	97$^1/_4$	4.6%	4.7%
Southern Railway 4s1956	86$^1/_2$	4.6%	4.9%
Union Pacific 4s1968	92$^3/_4$	4.3%	4.4%
Utilities			
Public Service E&G 4$^1/_2$s1970	102$^1/_2$	4.4%	4.4%
Other Industries			
Bethlehem Steel 5s1936	102	4.9%	4.6%
General Motors 6s1937	101$^1/_2$	5.9%	5.7%
Standard Oil of N.J. 5s1946	104$^5/_8$	4.8%	4.6%

Table 5.5: Selected bond prices at market close, December 31, 1930 [77]

Chapter 6

Jan.-Apr. 1931: Green Shoots of Spring

The beginning of 1931 was a period of modest revival in the economy. Production picked up, bank failures subsided, and stock prices moved upward. Many prominent business and political leaders predicted an imminent recovery [5, pp. 92-95].

However, an economic pickup was to be expected in the spring, and the spring revival of 1931 was in fact much smaller than a year earlier [5, p. 91] (Figures 4.1 and 4.2).

6.1   Financial Markets

Stock prices moved higher at the start of 1931 after hitting multi-year lows near the end of 1930 (Figure 6.1). Anticipation of recovery in the spring or summer brought many buyers into the market, causing stock prices to rise 18% in the first two months of the year. Bond prices rose as well, reducing the costs of borrowing [80]. The rally was purely speculative, however; by the end of February, many stocks had price/earnings ratios that exceeded those of 1929, since earnings for 1930 had dropped precipitously [81].

The stock rally peaked on February 24 with the Dow reaching 194.36 (Table 6.1) [82]. With investors disappointed by developments, stocks dropped substantially by April, falling below their levels at the start of the year (Table 6.2) [90].

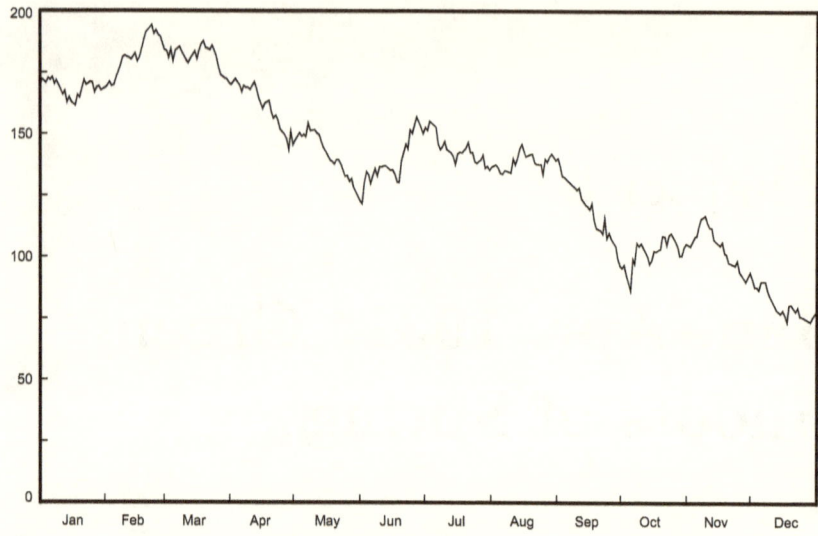

Figure 6.1: Dow Jones Industrial Average, 1931 [16]

Bond markets retained strength through March for high-grade issues; new issues of New York Central R.R. and Pennsylvania R.R. bonds on March 10 were fully subscribed within two hours [86]. However, bond prices fell steadily throughout April as well [93].

6.2   Bank Failures

With the economic pickup, bank suspensions abated considerably. The money supply correspondingly began to grow slightly (Figure 6.2) after dropping in the last two months of 1930.

Starting in March, bank runs began to gradually increase again. As more bank deposits were suspended, the money supply started declining. The rate of decline was fairly slow at first, but it would become steadily faster as the year went on. Friedman and Schwartz label March 1931 as the start of the "second banking crisis" [21, p. 313], but the data do not show levels of bank failures that are anywhere near comparable to the October-December 1930 crisis until at least June (Figures 5.10 and 5.11).

As with the first banking crisis of October-December 1930, there are no

Company	Stock Price	%YTD	Annual Dividend Rate		Dividend Yield
TUESDAY, FEBRUARY 24, 1931					
Agricultural Equipment					
Case (J.I.) & Co.	129³/₈	+44.8%	6		4.6%
International Harvester	58	+16.0%	2.50		4.3%
Autos					
Auburn Auto	209	+96.7%	4	+8% stk	1.9%
General Motors	44¹/₈	+24.7%	3		6.8%
Foods					
Coca-Cola	169	+15.8%	7.25†		4.3%
General Foods	54¹/₈	+10.5%	3		5.5%
Hershey Chocolate	95	+8.0%	5		5.3%
National Biscuit	83¹/₄	+7.2%	2.80		3.4%
Mining					
Anaconda Copper	42¹/₈	+40.4%	2.50		5.9%
Colorado Fuel & Iron	30¹/₂	+41.9%	1		3.3%
Kennecott Copper	31¹/₈	+33.9%	2		6.4%
Railroads					
New York Central	131¹/₄	+14.6%	8		6.1%
Pennsylvania R.R.	63	+12.0%	4		6.3%
Southern Pacific	107	+14.1%	6		5.6%
Southern Railway	62⁷/₈	+23.9%	8		12.7%
Union Pacific	204	+13.3%	10		4.9%
Retail					
Safeway Stores	58	+41.9%	5		8.6%
Sears Roebuck	58⁵/₈	+29.9%	2.50	+4% stk	4.3%
Woolworth	63³/₈	+14.2%	2.40		3.8%
Steel					
Bethlehem Steel	68¹/₄	+35.1%	6		8.8%
U.S. Steel	149³/₈	+7.4%	7		4.7%
Utilities					
Public Service, N. J.	87¹/₄	+17.1%	3.40		3.9%
Southern Cal. Edison	53	+15.2%	2		3.8%
Other Industries					
American Tobacco, B	120	+13.1%	6†		5.0%
General Electric	53³/₄	+23.2%	1.60		3.0%
Radio Corporation	26¹/₂	+120.8%	0		0.0%
Standard Oil of N. J.	51⁷/₈	+10.1%	2†		3.9%
United Aircraft & Tr	35³/₈	+47.4%	0		0.0%
† – includes extra dividend					

Table 6.1: Selected stock prices at market close, February 24, 1931 [83]

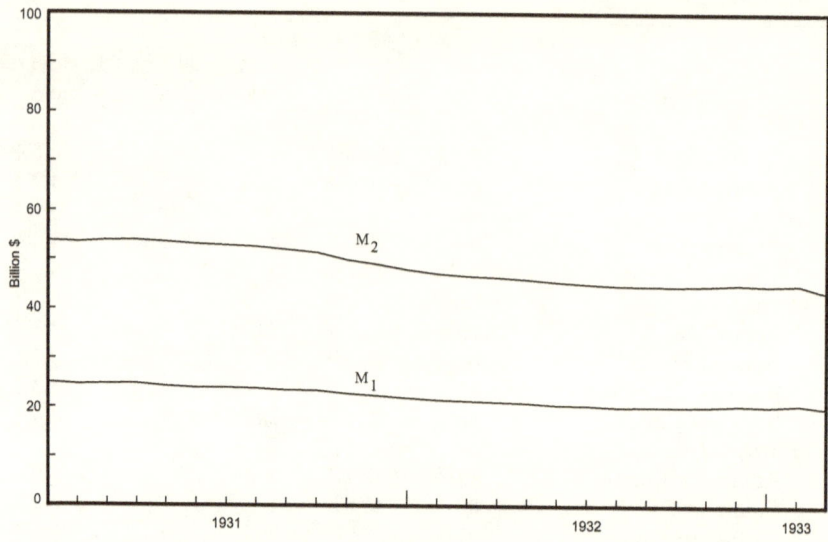

Figure 6.2: United States money supply, 1931 - 1933 [21]

indications of any great demand for gold at this point (Figures 6.3 and 6.4). Confidence in the banks was slowly eroding, particularly in rural areas, but the currency continued to be trusted as a store of value; Americans and foreigners alike retained confidence that the U.S. government would honor its obligation to redeem dollars for gold at $20.67 per ounce.

6.3   End of Agricultural Price Supports

On March 22, the Federal Farm Board finally pulled the plug on the price support program for wheat. Prices would continue to be supported until May 1931 for the 1930 crop, but no supports would be made afterward. July wheat at Chicago was already selling at $62\frac{1}{4}$¢/bushel before the announcement – over 20¢/bushel less than the supported May wheat price. The Grain Stabilization Corporation already held 100,000,000 bushels of wheat by this time and was expected to have 200,000,000 bushels by July in order to maintain the price supports for the 1930 crop [87], [88], [89].

Much damage to the wheat markets had been done by this time. The attempts by the federal policymakers to deny reality over the preceding

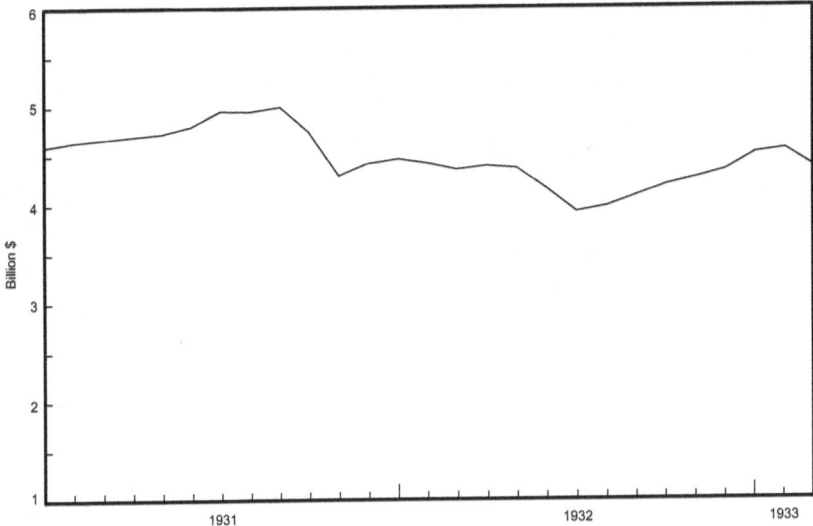

Figure 6.3: United States monetary gold stock, 1931 - 1933, including gold coin in circulation [12]

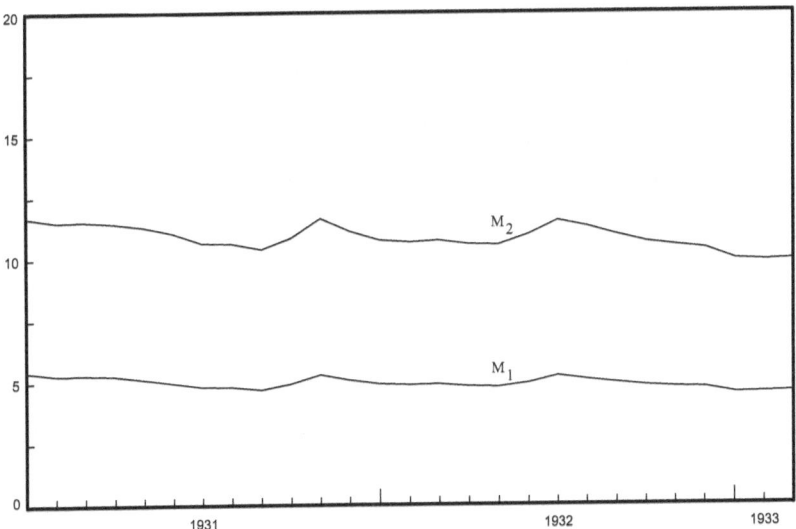

Figure 6.4: Ratio of money supply to monetary gold stock, 1931 - 1933

two years only made the situation much worse. The crop surpluses had already become huge by this point, and more had been planted in the expectation of further price supports [5, p. 105]. Ultimately, prices would end up being much lower than if supports hadn't been implemented in the first place, and consequently more producers would be wiped out due to the market "overswing." Besides the worldwide trade war, mechanization of farming in the 1920s [54] meant that a significant portion of farm labor could (and needed to) be redeployed to more productive jobs elsewhere in the economy [253, pp. 133-134].

The Federal Farm Board price supports avoided immediate price crashes, but at a consequence of a long period of declining prices and growing surpluses that hung over the market and discouraged any buying. Such a situation only made the inevitable price break much worse. This example illustrates well how the threat of a price break is worse than the price break itself [253, p. 72].

6.4   More Government Spending

When the government spending increases in FY 1930-31 turned out to be ineffectual, the politicians naturally chose to try a bigger dose of the same medicine. Appropriations passed in the last session of the 71st Congress (which adjourned March 3) would ultimately generate a 30% increase in spending for FY 1931-32 over FY 1930-31 (Figure 2.9) [261]. With prices still falling, the increase was 46% in real terms and 62% when expressed as a fraction of GNP. Expenditures for veterans bonus loans, drought relief, farm relief (including the Federal Farm Board), and "public construction to stimulate employment" accounted for much of the increase in spending [91]. The spending was financed by borrowing, which at least avoided a crippling tax hike (a mistake they'd make a year later). However, with an $800 million deficit looming, tax increases in the next session of Congress (starting in December) were increasingly expected [92, 102, 103].

State and local government spending remained the same in dollars for 1931 as for 1930 ($8.9 billion). However, this meant an 11.6% increase in real terms and an 11.5% share of GNP (19% larger than 1930).

THURSDAY, APRIL 30, 1931				
Company	Stock Price	%YTD	Annual Dividend Rate	Dividend Yield
Agricultural Equipment				
Case (J.I.) & Co.	83³/₄	−6.3%	6	7.2%
International Harvester	49¹/₂	−1.0%	2.50	5.1%
Autos				
Auburn Auto	213	+100.5%	4 +8% stk	1.9%
General Motors	41	+15.9%	3	7.3%
Foods				
Coca-Cola	148	+1.4%	7.25†	4.9%
General Foods	50³/₄	+3.6%	3	5.9%
Hershey Chocolate	95	+8.0%	5	5.3%
National Biscuit	71¹/₄	−8.2%	2.80	3.9%
Mining				
Anaconda Copper	30¹/₂	+1.7%	1.50	4.9%
Colorado Fuel & Iron	17	−20.9%	0	0.0%
Kennecott Copper	21³/₄	−6.5%	2	9.2%
Railroads				
New York Central	99¹/₄	−13.3%	6	6.0%
Pennsylvania R.R.	53³/₄	−4.4%	4	7.4%
Southern Pacific	89³/₄	−4.3%	6	6.7%
Southern Railway	40¹/₄	−20.7%	8	19.9%
Union Pacific	170¹/₈	−5.5%	10	5.9%
Retail				
Safeway Stores	52¹/₄	+27.8%	5	9.6%
Sears Roebuck	51⁷/₈	+15.0%	2.50 +4% stk	4.8%
Woolworth	61³/₈	+10.6%	2.40	3.9%
Steel				
Bethlehem Steel	43³/₈	−14.1%	4	9.2%
U.S. Steel	120	−13.7%	7	5.8%
Utilities				
Public Service, N. J.	82	+10.1%	3.40	4.1%
Southern Cal. Edison	45	−2.2%	2	4.4%
Other Industries				
American Tobacco, B	125¹/₂	+18.3%	6†	4.8%
General Electric	43⁷/₈	+0.6%	1.60	3.6%
Radio Corporation	16³/₄	+39.6%	0	0.0%
Standard Oil of N. J.	37³/₈	−20.7%	2†	5.4%
United Aircraft & Tr	28¹/₈	+17.2%	0	0.0%
† − includes extra dividend				

Table 6.2: Selected stock prices at market close, April 30, 1931 [94]

Chapter 7

May 1931: The First Domino

In May 1931, the collapse of Austria's largest private bank started a wave of financial crises that would sweep across Europe over the next several months. Austria's small gold reserves amounted to only $1/30$ of the money supply. Thus, it is not surprising that the first major European currency crisis of the Great Depression occurred there. A decade of monetary strain unleashed a chain of "financial contagion" – transmitted via inflated currencies – that was not yet apparent to most contemporary commentators.

7.1 Austria's "Consumption of Capital"

Excessive consumption since the start of World War I was the root of the Austrian financial collapse of 1931 [253, pp. 91-92], [36]. With a large list of "progressive" social benefits – compulsory illness insurance, accident insurance, unemployment insurance, unemployment benefits, pensions for the elderly – municipal public expenditures per capita nearly quadrupled from 1923 to 1929 (Figure 7.1). Federal government expenditures per capita also doubled over this time (Figure 7.2). Real wages increased by over 60%, leading to much unemployment (Figure 7.3). Consumption in Austria was in excess of production; it was paid for by a steady reduction in capital [36].

Capital gradually loses value over time. This loss of value occurs in a number of ways. Virtually all capital requires some sort of maintenance;

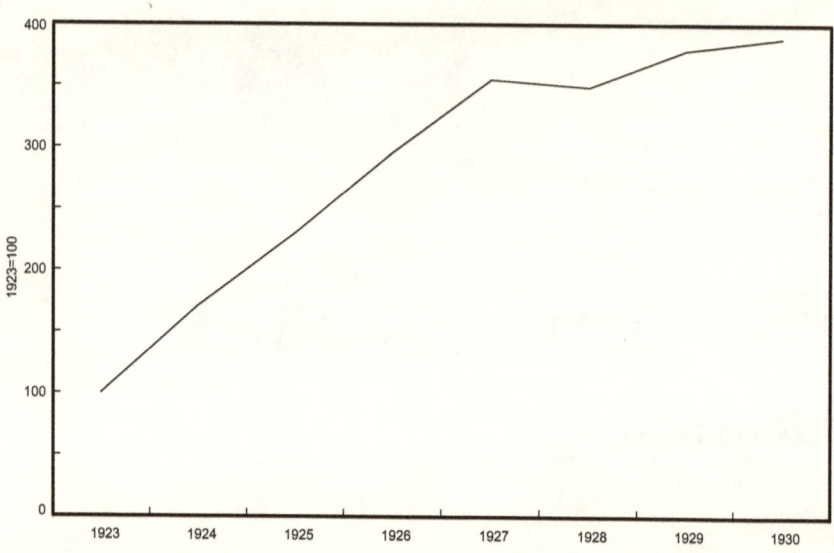

Figure 7.1: Austrian municipality expenditures per capita, 1923 - 1930 [36]

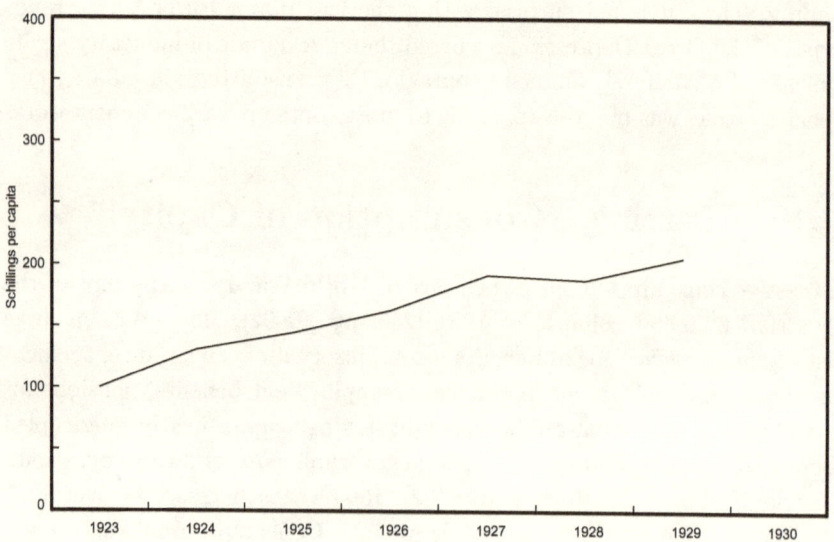

Figure 7.2: Austrian federal government expenditures per capita, 1923 - 1930 [36]

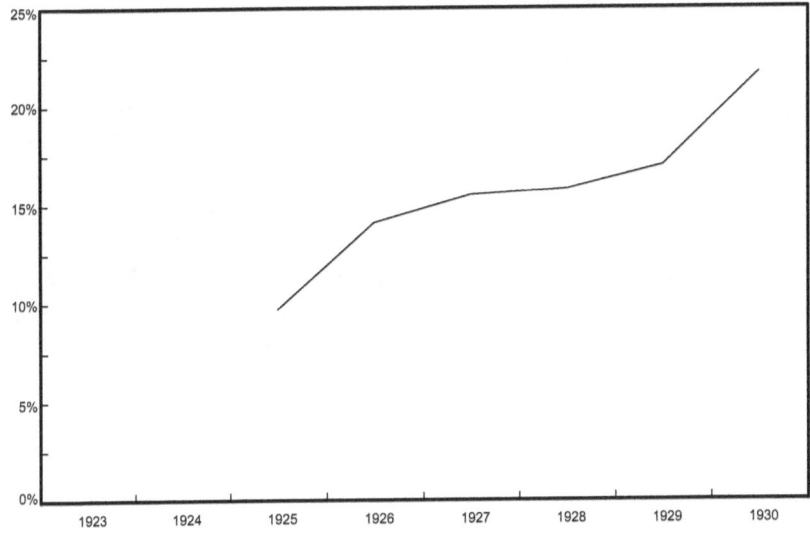

Figure 7.3: Austrian unemployment rate, 1923 - 1930 [36]

without it, the capital loses its productivity and hence its value. A state of the art factory can become obsolete in a matter of a few years as newer production techniques are developed over time. Since improved productivity lowers prices, older, less efficient plants are no longer able to compete or produce enough to meet their costs. Consumer preferences can also change over time, devaluing existing capital. A steady infusion of investment is therefore required to simply preserve the value of existing capital; additional investment is needed to increase it [36].

Austria's high consumption levels were essentially subsidized by funds that would otherwise have been used to maintain and replace capital. A combination of taxes, trade union actions, inflation, and protective tariffs all served to inhibit maintenance of existing capital or investment in new capital. Since productive capacity was not maintained, it fell steadily over an 18-year period. An analysis of corporations listed on the Viennese stock exchange in 1930 by the Austrian Institut für Konjunkturforschung (Institute for Business Cycle Research) indicates that the collective value of corporate capital remaining in post-war Austria declined by a staggering 79% from 1913 to 1930. By October 1931, the decline reached 87% [36].

7.2   Kreditanstalt in Austria

By 1931, Austria's financial situation was so shaky that the country was dependent on foreign credit to stay afloat. Crisis had been postponed in 1929 when the relatively healthy Österreichische Kreditanstalt absorbed the failing Bodenkreditanstalt to form the Kreditanstalt für Handel und Gewerbe [254, p. 257]. On Monday, May 11, an advance of 160,000,000 schillings ($23,000,000) to the Kreditanstalt was announced, with 100,000,000 schillings coming from the Austrian government, 30,000,000 schillings from the Austrian National Bank, and 30,000,000 schillings from the Rothschild banking house, who were the Kreditanstalt's principal shareholders. The Kreditanstalt, Austria's largest private bank, effectively owned 80% of Austria's industry. The bank had losses of 140,000,000 schillings which were made public that day. The size of these losses was not publicly expected, and without the advance, the bank likely would have closed within 24 hours. The bank had share capital of 125,000,000 schillings and 40,000,000 schillings of open reserves; thus, the bank reportedly could have met its liabilities, but its shareholders would have been virtually wiped out, and $3/4$ of Austrian industry would have come to a halt. As part of the deal, the original share capital was reduced by 25% (31,000,000 schillings). Even with the advance, a steady stream of depositors began withdrawing their cash [95, 100, 118].

The advance to the Kreditanstalt effectively transferred the liabilities of the Kreditanstalt from the bank to Austria's currency. In order to back its commitment to the Kreditanstalt, the Austrian government needed to borrow money from abroad. Parliament approved a foreign loan of 150,000,000 schillings in the early morning (12:45 AM) of May 14. There was contentious debate about bailing out the shareholders (the Socialists wanted the share capital reduced by 80% instead of 25%), but the governing coalition did not want foreign investors to lose heavily, fearing an end to future investment [98]. Since Austria had borrowed heavily from abroad in 1922 to recover from its hyperinflationary collapse, Austria needed approval of this additional loan from the Control Committee of the nations that guaranteed the 1922 loan [96, 97]. This approval was granted the following week [107]; however, that action did not assure that anyone would actually loan Austria the money. With suitable authority obtained, the Austrian National Bank sought to float 150,000,000 schillings of three-year treasury bonds to stabilize the financial situation [101].

On May 18, the Bank for International Settlements (World Bank) announced that it would make a three-month, 100,000,000 schilling credit available to the Austrian National Bank on request. This announcement was intended to calm fears and prevent a panic in Austria. Ominously, however, the same bank stated that it could not assist in the purchase of the Austrian 3-year treasury bonds. The reason for this rejection was political – Austria was seeking to form a customs union with Germany, and France staunchly opposed this move [254, pp. 257-258], [101], [99]. A number of announcements of additional financial assistance and agreements to purchase the Austrian bonds followed over the next several weeks [107, 109, 116, 117], but no significant hard currency was actually provided. France had accumulated large gold reserves over several years from the undervaluation of the franc, and France was unwilling to provide financial assistance to Austria unless Austria abandoned the customs union with Germany [112].

During the following weeks, a steady stream of nervous depositors withdrew their cash from the Kreditanstalt. In order to stay open, the Kreditanstalt began to call in as many loans as it could. These actions led to the failure of another Austrian bank, the Auspitz Lieben Bank, which had become dependent on Kreditanstalt credit to survive after it suffered several speculative losses in the 1920s [105, 260].

On May 26, it was reported that the Kreditanstalt was in need of additional cash to meet foreign claims. By this time, depositors had withdrawn a large amount of funds, leaving the bank in short supply of money [104]. On May 29, Parliament authorized a government guarantee of all new liabilities of the bank without any limit – only the Heimwehr party voted against this measure. The guarantee was needed to persuade foreign bankers to support the Kreditanstalt and maintain their credits there. The liabilities guaranteed were thought to possibly be as much as 1.2 billion schillings, adding greatly to the burden borne by the currency. This second crisis was triggered largely by French threats to withdraw from the Kreditanstalt their short-term credits, which were due at the end of the month. American short-term credits were reportedly withdrawn at the end of the month as well [106, 107, 111], a claim which was later found to be false [119].

7.3 United States

In the U.S., May proved to be another month of steady market declines. Despite a reduction in the New York Federal Reserve discount rate from 2%

to $1\frac{1}{2}$% on May 8 – the lowest central bank rate in recorded world history up to that time [203, 204] – the Dow fell to a new multi-year low of 128.46 at the end of the month. The significance of the Austrian financial crisis was not apparent in the press; stories about it only made the front page of the New York Times once (May 19) [101]. Investors, however, may have taken the situation more seriously; declines were larger in the American securities markets than in Europe [108].

Chapter 8

June 1931: Hoover's Offer of Grace

After the Dow fell to a six-year low of 121.70 on June 2 (Table 8.1), the markets rallied later in the month when President Hoover spoke of the need to postpone payments on outstanding intergovernmental debts from World War I. These debts had become burdensome in the presence of steadily falling prices (a consequence of declining international trade) and contributed significantly to economic instability.

8.1 Austrian Crisis

The Austrian financial situation remained uncertain as June began. The World Bank arranged a 100,000,000 schilling credit in concert with ten central banks to provide liquidity for Austrian depositors by converting Austrian loans into cash [107, 109, 117], but no gold-backed currency had been provided to support the 160,000,000 schilling advance to the Kreditanstalt. The Austrian National Bank rate was raised from 5% to 6% on June 6 and $7\frac{1}{2}$% on June 15 [111], [118]. Negotiations between the Austrian government, led by Chancellor Otto Ender, and foreign creditors, represented by Sir Robert Kindersley of the Bank of England and James H. Gannon of Chase National Bank of New York, culminated in an agreement on June 16 in which the foreign bankers agreed to continue their short term loans with Austria for an additional two years. In return, the Austrian govern-

TUESDAY, JUNE 2, 1931				
Company	Stock Price	%YTD	Annual Dividend Rate	Dividend Yield
Agricultural Equipment				
Case (J.I.) & Co.	63³/₈	−29.1%	6	9.5%
International Harvester	39³/₄	−20.5%	2.50	6.3%
Autos				
Auburn Auto	138	+29.9%	4 +8% stk	2.9%
General Motors	31¹/₂	−11.0%	3	9.5%
Foods				
Coca-Cola	136¹/₂	−6.5%	7.50†	5.5%
General Foods	43⁷/₈	−10.5%	3	6.8%
Hershey Chocolate	84¹/₄	−4.3%	5	5.9%
National Biscuit	60¹/₄	−22.4%	2.80	4.6%
Mining				
Anaconda Copper	19³/₈	−35.4%	1.50	7.7%
Colorado Fuel & Iron	10¹/₈	−52.9%	0	0.0%
Kennecott Copper	14⁵/₈	−37.1%	1	6.8%
Railroads				
New York Central	71³/₄	−37.3%	6	8.4%
Pennsylvania R.R.	42³/₈	−24.7%	4	9.4%
Southern Pacific	67¹/₄	−28.3%	6	8.9%
Southern Railway	27¹/₈	−46.6%	8	29.5%
Union Pacific	137¹/₈	−23.8%	10	7.3%
Retail				
Safeway Stores	45¹/₂	+11.3%	5	11.0%
Sears Roebuck	46¹/₈	+2.2%	2.50 +4% stk	5.4%
Woolworth	63¹/₈	+13.7%	2.40	3.8%
Steel				
Bethlehem Steel	39³/₈	−22.0%	4	10.2%
U.S. Steel	83³/₈	−40.1%	7	8.4%
Utilities				
Public Service, N. J.	73¹/₂	−1.3%	3.40	4.6%
Southern Cal. Edison	38¹/₂	−16.3%	2	5.2%
Other Industries				
American Tobacco, B	104	−2.0%	6†	5.8%
General Electric	36⁵/₈	−16.0%	1.60	4.4%
Radio Corporation	13³/₈	+11.5%	0	0.0%
Standard Oil of N. J.	30⁵/₈	−35.0%	2†	6.5%
United Aircraft & Tr	22¹/₂	−6.2%	0	0.0%
† – includes extra dividend				

Table 8.1: Selected stock prices at market close, June 2, 1931 [110]

ment agreed to guarantee the foreign liabilities of the Kreditanstalt, which totaled about 500,000,000 schillings. Interior Minister Franz Winkler quit his post in opposition to the deal, and the entire remainder of the Cabinet resigned as soon as the agreement was signed. As a representative of the Farmer's party, Winkler's resignation meant a loss of confidence in the Cabinet by one of the parties of the governing coalition [119].

The next day (June 17), the Bank of England provided a 150,000,000 schilling advance to Austria, finally providing the hard currency needed to back the Kreditanstalt advance of May 11. This advance was a short-term loan, but it was expected to be renewed until the 150,000,000 schillings of Austrian Treasury bonds were issued [122]. French conditions for providing financial assistance were deemed to be intolerable and humiliating by the Austrians, and thus the British felt compelled to step in [123, 128, 129]. A new Cabinet was formed on June 20 by Dr. Karl Buresch, the Governor of Lower Austria [125]. A collapse appeared to be averted, and the political and financial situation in Austria stabilized for the time being.

The government extended its guarantee of Kreditanstalt debts to the domestic liabilities of the bank on June 26. This action increased the amount of liabilities guaranteed by the government to 1 billion schillings. Foreign creditors had been urging that this step be taken to calm depositor fears and prevent the large withdrawals that had taken place by this time [131].

8.2 Germany

Although Germany was not heavily invested in Austria, the Kreditanstalt crisis precipitated a lack of confidence in German investments. Foreign investors began to question the safety of their investments in Germany, and a run on banks in Germany commenced [253, pp. 92-93]. Many foreign investors believed that German banks were in a similarly precarious situation and that German banks were themselves heavily invested in the Kreditanstalt, despite emphatic statements from the Reichsbank to the contrary[1]. Large withdrawals of gold and foreign currency started on June 2 [218] and reached 150,000,000 marks per day on June 12 [115]. By June 13, these withdrawals totaled 835,000,000 marks ($200,400,000) for the month, when the Reichsbank raised its bank rate from 5% to 7% [115]. This action

---

[1]However, like Austria, a considerable amount of investment had not been directed into productive capital [253, pp. 8-9], [256, p. 117]. Also, trade barriers worldwide blocked German exports, reducing their value [5, pp. 219-220].

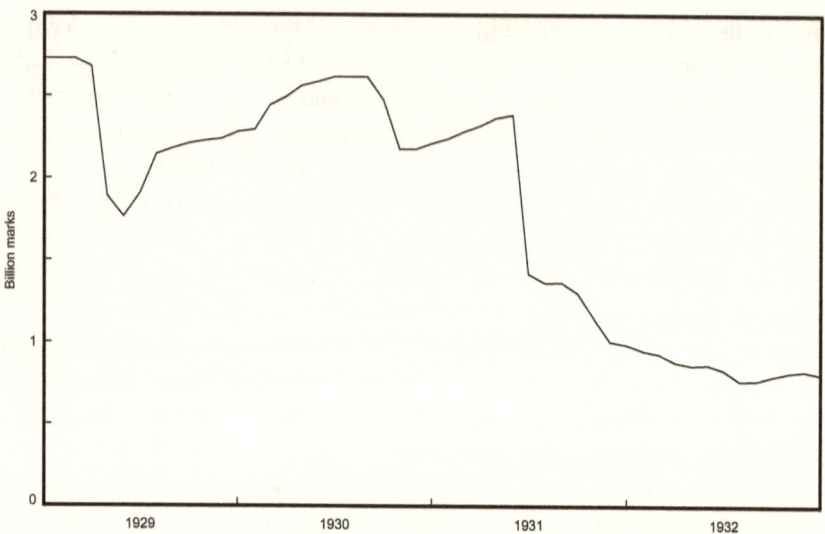

Figure 8.1: German central bank gold reserves, 1929 - 1932 [12]

slowed the withdrawals, but the drain continued for the remainder of the month (Figure 8.1).

On June 25, a 400,000,000 mark ($100,000,000) short-term credit was extended to Germany by four major banks: the Bank of England, the Bank of France, the U.S. Federal Reserve, and the Bank for International Settlements. The loan was expected to last just a few weeks so that Germany would have sufficient cash to deal with temporary end-of-month demands for currency [130].

8.3 Hoover Moratorium

On Saturday, June 20, Hoover issued a statement proposing a one-year suspension of principal and interest payments on intergovernmental debts owed to the United States (Table 8.2) for the fiscal year 1931-32 (from July 1, 1931 to June 30, 1932). The U.S. was scheduled to receive a total of $246,600,000 in such payments ($62,300,000 in principal and $184,200,000 in interest) during this time. The suspension was conditioned on a like suspension of intergovernmental debts (including German reparations) owed

Nation	Remaining Principal (million $)	1931 National Product(million $)	Debt/Product Ratio
Belgium	401	12,800 (NNP)	3%
Britain	4,398	18,980 (GDP)	23%
France	3,864	11,712 (GDP)	33%
Italy	2,005	5,840 (GNP)	34%
Others	267	-	-
Total	5,400	-	-

Table 8.2: War debts owed to United States after World War I [27, 39]

to the nations that were in debt to the U.S. Private debts were not covered [124]. The moratorium was intended to spur an economic recovery by temporarily removing these burdens, and the worsening financial situation in Germany prompted Hoover to act [127, 135]. The moratorium would relieve Germany of about $427,200,000 in reparations and other payments due for 1931-32. Hoover reiterated the American policy that war debts owed to the United States were not contingent on reparations – reparations were regarded as a strictly European issue – and that the debts would not be cancelled. Hoover also indicated that countries that reduced military spending would receive favorable consideration from the U.S. on debt modifications [124].

Several Congressmen from both political parties spoke favorably about Hoover's proposal. Although Hoover's proposal required Congressional action to be implemented, Hoover did not call for a special session of Congress, even though Congress would not return to regular session until early December, which was just a few days before the next debt installment date of December 15. Hoover evidently believed that Congress would quickly take action on the moratorium at that time. There was speculation that a special session might begin developing a variety of other legislation that Hoover opposed [124].

Many world leaders cheered the Hoover Moratorium. British officials in particular spoke very highly of Hoover's initiative, even though the plan would be a net loss for their country – for the year, Britain owed $161,100,000 in debt payments but was scheduled to receive $180,700,000. The British generally recognized that a German economic collapse would be catastrophic for them as well (this proved to be true). They also believed that the one-year moratorium would be extended [127].

French reaction was much more muted – France owed $104,800,000 for the year covered by the moratorium but was scheduled to receive $201,500,000. France was also clearly apprehensive about a strengthened German economy [127]. Nevertheless, France agreed in principle to the Hoover Moratorium on July 6. Some details regarding German payments that were due under the Young Plan remained to be worked out [136].

The markets rallied sharply after Hoover's announcement. The Dow Jones average rose 8.65 points to 138.96 on June 20 (Table 8.3) and another 6.86 points to 145.82 on June 22 – an increase of almost 12% over the two days. The rally continued toward the end of the month.

8.4 Bank Failures

After gradually rising since March, bank failures spiked in June, with $190,000,000 in deposits at suspended banks [13]. The failures were mainly a continuation of the crises that had started during the previous autumn. A wave of 19 bank suspensions occurred on June 8 and 9 in the Chicago metropolitan area [114]. The wave was stemmed when stronger banks in the area agreed to guarantee the deposits of the smaller banks [132].

A significant inflow of gold into the United States was reported for the first half of 1931. This inflow was the result of a number of things, including repayments of earlier foreign loans (that were no longer being extended) and a monetary contraction from the many bank failures and deposit withdrawals [171], [21, p. 342]. The inflow was particularly pronounced in June, when semi-annual payments on the war debt issues were due. The continuing gold inflow indicated that great confidence remained in U.S. currency.

The continuing bank failures, therefore, both strengthened and weakened the currency. By contracting the money supply and imposing losses on depositors, the bank failures increased the gold backing of the remaining dollars. (This statement is not arguing in any way that the losses were imposed equitably – see Chapter 1). However, the failures were clearly detrimental to confidence, leading to further withdrawals and liquidity demands, thus bringing the currency closer to a gold crisis.

SATURDAY, JUNE 20, 1931					
NYSE Volume: 1,508,105 shares					
Company	Last	Change	%YTD	Dividend	
Agricultural Equipment					
Case (J.I.) & Co.	$72^1/_4$	$+7^7/_8$	−19.2%	6	
International Harvester	$41^7/_8$	$+2^3/_8$	−16.2%	2.50	
Autos					
Auburn Auto	169	$+16^3/_4$	+59.1%	4	+8% stk
General Motors	$35^5/_8$	$+2^1/_4$	+0.7%	3	
Foods					
General Foods	$48^1/_4$	$+1^3/_4$	−1.5%	3	
Hershey Chocolate	$92^1/_2$	+2	+5.1%	5	
National Biscuit	$66^5/_8$	$+3^7/_8$	−14.2%	2.80	
Mining					
Anaconda Copper	$23^3/_8$	$+2^5/_8$	−22.1%	1.50	
Kennecott Copper	$18^3/_8$	+2	−21.0%	1	
Railroads					
New York Central	$89^1/_2$	$+6^7/_8$	−21.8%	6	
Pennsylvania R.R.	$48^3/_4$	$+2^3/_4$	−13.3%	4	
Southern Pacific	80	+3	−14.7%	6	
Southern Railway	35	+3	−31.0%	6	
Union Pacific	162	+10	−10.0%	10	
Retail					
Safeway Stores	51	+2	+24.8%	5	
Sears Roebuck	$53^1/_4$	$+2^7/_8$	+18.0%	2.50	
Woolworth	$68^1/_4$	$+2^1/_2$	+23.0%	2.40	
Steel					
Bethlehem Steel	$44^7/_8$	$+3^1/_2$	−11.1%	4	
U.S. Steel	$92^7/_8$	+6	−33.2%	7	
Utilities					
Public Service, N. J.	$82^1/_2$	$+3^5/_8$	+10.7%	3.40	
Southern Cal. Edison	$42^3/_4$	+1	−7.1%	2	
Other Industries					
American Tobacco, B	113	$+2^5/_8$	+6.5%	6†	
General Electric	$42^1/_4$	$+4^1/_8$	−3.2%	1.60	
Radio Corporation	16	$+1^5/_8$	+33.3%	0	
Standard Oil of N. J.	37	+2	−21.5%	2†	
United Aircraft & Tr	$26^3/_4$	$+3^3/_8$	+11.5%	0	
† – includes extra dividend					

Table 8.3: Selected stock prices at market close, June 20, 1931 [126]

Chapter 9

July-Aug. 1931: A Cascade of Crises

The enthusiasm of the Moratorium Rally faded as further financial crises blossomed throughout Europe (Tables 9.1 and 9.2).

9.1 Financial Crisis in Germany

The financial situation continued to worsen in Germany as July began. Over 40,000,000 marks of foreign exchange was withdrawn on Friday, July 3, and another 30,000,000 marks was withdrawn the next day [135]. Even French acceptance of the Hoover Moratorium on July 6 [136] did little to inspire confidence in foreign investors, and heavy withdrawals continued. On July 7, private industry in Germany offered to collectively guarantee the liabilities of the Gold Discount Bank, a subsidiary of the Reichsbank. The initial guarantee was set at 500,000,000 marks. This guarantee was made binding by the German government the next day on any firm with a capitalization of at least 5,000,000 marks. The objective of the guarantee was to make the Gold Discount Bank a "clearing house for foreign credits" [137].

Hans Luther, president of the Reichsbank, met with Montagu Norman (Governor of the Bank of England) and Clément Moret (Governor of the Bank of France) in an attempt to secure a new foreign loan for Germany. The amount sought was reported to be around 2 billion marks. Currency withdrawals continued, reaching 50,000,000 marks on July 9. Gold backing of the mark had fallen close to the legal limit of 40% of the banknotes in circulation. Currency was pulled out of circulation to maintain this backing. By this time, Germany had lost 1.5 billion marks of gold and foreign currency in five weeks [138].

The crisis came to a head on July 13, when the Darmstaedter und Nationalbank (Danat Bank) shut down operations. 1,000,000,000 marks – 40% of its credits – had been withdrawn since June 1930. Of this total, 100,000,000 marks were withdrawn in May, 300,000,000 in June, and 250,000,000 in the first two weeks of July. In an ominous harbinger of things to come, anti-Semitic agitation against the bank had been published by the National Socialist press [139]. Ironically, one of the major supporters of the Nazis had his assets frozen by the Danat Bank's failure [140].

The other major banks in Germany immediately restricted withdrawals to a maximum of 10%, while the German government announced a guarantee of 100% of the Danat Bank's deposits. The German Boerse (stock exchange) suspended operations – although a two day suspension was announced, the exchange would remain closed for nearly two months. In all, 2,000,000,000 marks of foreign credits had been withdrawn from Germany in the preceding 2½ months [139].

The shock waves of the German crisis were felt throughout central Europe the next day (July 14). A two-day bank holiday was declared in Germany [140]. Banks in Hungary were closed by the government for three days. A $25,000,000 foreign credit to Hungary had not been received – the delay was attributed to the German crisis. Latvian banks also suspended payments, and banks in Danzig limited payments to 10%. Interestingly, Austrian banks remained open, except for the Mercurbank in Vienna, which was owned mostly by the Danat Bank and had suffered "something like a run" [142]. Private business and exchanges refused to accept German marks in many European countries – Switzerland, Sweden, Denmark, Czechoslovakia, Belgium – stranding many German travelers abroad [142].

An agreement to limit Germany's unconditional reparations payment[1] to 41,000,000 marks, with 36,000,000 marks immediately loaned back to Germany by the Bank for International Settlements, eased tensions somewhat [143]. Also, the 400,000,000 mark credit was renewed on July 14 for

---

[1] Germany still owed the unconditional portion of the reparations payments under the Young Plan to France as part of the deal to obtain French acceptance of the Hoover Moratorium.

another month, in recognition of the reality that Germany could not repay it. At the same time, it was generally acknowledged that any additional loans to Germany would require a conference of political leaders, as central banks would not be willing to extend further credit to Germany under the existing conditions [141].

July 15 saw considerable volatility in the currency exchange markets. The pound sterling dropped nearly 2 full cents to $4.83½ as doubts about the gold backing of the pound increased following England's financial support of central Europe. The French franc jumped 1⁷⁄₁₆¢ to 3.93⁷⁄₈¢ – above the gold export point.[2] German checks were honored by U.S. banks [145]. The Reichsbank raised its discount rate from 7% to 10%. Also on July 15, Communist riots broke out in many German cities, but they were quelled by the police [144].

The banks reopened on July 16 as promised, but with strict controls on currency withdrawals and foreign exchange. Although the mark was still nominally valued at ¹⁄₂₇₉₀ kg of gold, or 23.82 cents, the exchange restrictions meant that Germany was in effect no longer on a gold standard [144], [148], [253, pp. 100-102].

On July 18, a government emergency decree stated that all Germans were required to declare all of their foreign exchange holdings to the Reichsbank for conversion to German currency on demand. The penalty for noncompliance was imprisonment up to 10 years. German banks agreed to guarantee each other's deposits [151].

A London conference of high-level delegates from seven nations, including German Chancellor Heinrich Bruening, French Premier Pierre Laval, and British Prime Minister Ramsey MacDonald along with the U.S. Secretaries of State (Henry Stimson) and the Treasury (Andrew Mellon), concluded on July 23 with an agreement to extend the 400,000,000 mark credit an additional three months. At the insistence of the French, thorny issues such as reparations and the Austro-German customs union were left off of the agenda [152, 153]. On July 29, private American and British banks agreed to leave their short-term credits in Germany as well. The credits were to be transferred to the Gold Discount Bank so that they would receive the backing of German industry [156]. These agreements were a formal ac-

---

[2] Because of the fractional reserve banking system, exchange rates fluctuated between the currencies of different countries, even though the currencies were redeemable in a fixed weight of gold. Any significant deviation from par, however, would result in a massive flow of gold.

ceptance of the reality that these assets had become indefinitely frozen; there was no way that they all could be withdrawn, due to Germany's lack of hard currency [157].

The Reichsbank raised the discount rate again, from 10% to 15%, on the last day of July. This harsh medicine appeared to finally stabilize the situation somewhat, and the Reichsbank subsequently reduced the rate back to 10% on August 11 and to 8% on September 2 [218].

9.2   Agricultural Markets

The federal government issued updated agricultural forecasts on August 8 and August 10. The government's estimate of the cotton crop for 1931 was more than 10% larger than the average of previous private estimates, triggering a crash of more than 1¢/pound (over 12%) in cotton prices on exchanges around the world [158]. The wheat crop was predicted to be 3.5% larger than in 1930 and 2.8% larger than was forecast on July 1 [159]. Having already fallen sharply with the abandonment of Federal Farm Board supports, wheat prices remained relatively steady in response to the news over the next couple of months (Figure 5.3). Rye prices rallied somewhat as the revised forecast showed a drop in production over both the July 1 forecast and the 1930 crop [159], but corn prices dropped sharply in the second half of August (Figure 5.4).

9.3   Propping Up England

With England having loaned heavily to Germany and Austria, the Bank of England's gold was doing double duty backing German and Austrian currency as well as British pounds. With bleak prospects of renewed production in Germany and Austria, foreign investors became suspicious of the pound's value and started converting their pounds into gold and foreign currency at parity while they could.

The U.S. Federal Reserve and the Bank of France jointly extended a £50,000,000 credit (about $250,000,000) to the Bank of England on August 1 to support the value of the British pound sterling. Such aid had been rumored for several weeks, but Governor Montagu Norman of the Bank of England repeatedly denied it. Finally, a credit was accepted on August 1. The credit, like the Reichsbank credit, was an agreement by the

MONDAY, AUGUST 31, 1931				
Company	Stock Price	%YTD	Annual Dividend Rate	Dividend Yield
Agricultural Equipment				
Case (J.I.) & Co.	62¼	−30.3%	6	9.6%
International Harvester	38	−24.0%	2.50	6.6%
Autos				
Auburn Auto	134½	+26.6%	4 +8% stk	3.0%
General Motors	36	+1.8%	3	8.3%
Foods				
Coca-Cola	146	+0.0%	7.75†	5.3%
General Foods	50½	+3.1%	3	5.9%
National Biscuit	58⅛	−25.1%	2.80	4.8%
Mining				
Anaconda Copper	24¾	−17.5%	1.50	6.1%
Colorado Fuel & Iron	14	−34.9%	0	0.0%
Kennecott Copper	17⅜	−25.3%	1	5.8%
Railroads				
New York Central	69⅜	−39.4%	6	8.6%
Pennsylvania R.R.	39	−30.7%	3	7.7%
Southern Pacific	73⅝	−21.5%	6	8.1%
Southern Railway	25¼	−50.2%	6	23.8%
Union Pacific	144	−20.0%	10	6.9%
Retail				
Safeway Stores	65½	+60.2%	5	7.6%
Sears Roebuck	55½	+23.0%	2.50	4.5%
Woolworth	69⅝	+25.5%	2.40	3.4%
Steel				
Bethlehem Steel	39⅝	−21.5%	2	5.0%
U.S. Steel	87½	−37.1%	4	4.6%
Utilities				
Public Service, N. J.	80½	+8.1%	3.40	4.2%
Southern Cal. Edison	44	−4.3%	2	4.5%
Other Industries				
American Tobacco, B	111½	+5.1%	6†	5.4%
General Electric	40⅝	−6.9%	1.60	3.9%
Radio Corporation	19¾	+64.6%	0	0.0%
Standard Oil of N. J.	40½	−14.1%	2†	4.9%
United Aircraft & Tr	27½	+14.6%	0	0.0%
† – includes extra dividend				

Table 9.1: Selected stock prices at market close, August 31, 1931 [162]

Monday, August 31, 1931			
Company/Issue	Bond Price	Current Yield	Yield to Maturity
Railroads			
New York Central 5s2013	101¼	4.9%	4.9%
Pennsylvania R.R. 4½s1970	91⅜	4.9%	5.0%
Southern Pacific 4½s1968	85⅜	5.3%	5.4%
Southern Railway 4s1956	68¼	5.9%	6.6%
Union Pacific 4s1968	92	4.3%	4.4%
Utilities			
Public Service E&G 4½s1970	105	4.3%	4.2%
Other Industries			
Bethlehem Steel 5s1936	103¼	4.8%	4.3%
General Motors 6s1937	103	5.8%	5.4%
Standard Oil of N.J. 5s1946	104¾	4.8%	4.6%

Table 9.2: Selected bond prices at market close, August 31, 1931 [163]

American and French central banks to purchase sterling bills. The amount of £50,000,000 was expected to be more than sufficient to meet immediate liquidity demands and support the pound's value [34, 157], which was gradually recovering after its relative plunge on July 15.

The financial world was stunned by the news on August 24 that the £50,000,000 credit had been almost completely exhausted. It was generally believed that only about 20% of the credit had been used. £30,000,000 – one-sixth of England's gold stock – had been withdrawn in the previous three weeks [160]. An internal debate in the Cabinet over cuts to the unemployment dole was noted, as Britain was facing a £120,000,000 government deficit [160, 161]. The U.S. Federal Reserve and Bank of France hastily arranged an additional £80,000,000 ($400,000,000) loan on August 28 to further bolster the pound [161].

Chapter 10

Sept. 1931: Worldwide Financial Panic

The international monetary crisis reached a climax in September. The value of currencies and the credit of nations collapsed throughout the world after Britain's dramatic and abrupt announcement on September 20 that redemption of pounds for gold would be suspended. Most northern and central European nations followed suit within a week. Currency exchange rates fluctuated wildly. By the end of the month, a global scramble for gold was underway, with even the United States experiencing a significant run on its gold reserves.

Under these circumstances, where the value of currency is so uncertain, it becomes difficult (if not impossible) for buyers and sellers to agree on prices for transactions. The buyer will naturally think that the currency is worth more than the seller does. It should therefore not be surprising at all that the bottom fell out of the economy at this point and the normal seasonal autumn business revival did not even materialize [5, p. 115].

In the U.S., the stock market fell rapidly and nearly continuously throughout most of the month, driven by steep dividend cuts and cancellations. Foreign liquidation was also significant. The percentage decline for the month remains the largest in U.S. history to date. Bank suspensions soared, with banks in the large cities becoming threatened as well [21, pp. 315-317].

10.1   Stock Market Crash

The month of September began quietly on the New York Stock Exchange, with the lowest full-day trading volume (533,570 shares) in seven years [164]. The next day, stocks dropped significantly (Table 10.1) (the Dow Jones Industrial Average was down 3.82 points to 137.31), with railroads leading the decline after Lehigh Valley announced that no dividend would be paid and the weekly railroad freight report showed continued weakness [165].

On Thursday, September 3, the Dow Jones Industrial Average fell 4.17 points to 133.14 (Table 10.2) after J.I. Case Co., a farm equipment manufacturer [174], suspended its dividend. The company had been maintaining a $6 annual dividend rate. Analysts had expected a dividend cut of 50% or less. News of large drops in prices (25% to 40%) on the German Boerse, which resumed limited trading, were also noted by investors. Volume on the NYSE, although still very small in comparison to the 1929 crash, increased markedly to 2,131,510 shares – a large increase from the dull activity just two days earlier, and the highest daily volume since July 14. U.S. Steel hit a 9-year low [167, 168].

After a slight rally in some stocks on Friday and a three-day market holiday for Labor Day, stocks resumed their plunge on Tuesday, September 8, with the Dow Jones average down 3.43 points to 129.19. Many more dividend cuts and omissions were announced – although the actions were not really unexpected, the market nevertheless reacted sharply. A lack of seasonal increase in rail traffic was also noted, as rail shares reached ten-year lows. American steel production was the lowest since 1921 [172]. It was noted two days later [173] that while railroad salaries had been reduced, railroad wages had not changed since the start of the depression despite significant traffic declines. Another drop of 4.38 points came in the Dow Jones average on September 12.

By September 14, stock prices had clearly penetrated the "resistance level" of June 2, as noted by the Times [177]. (The Dow Jones was down 2.55 to 121.30 that day.) The declines came despite firm commodity prices, which overall had shown no significant movement for over 17 weeks [175]. Short interest was noted to be the highest since the latter part of May [177], and continued declines the next couple of days were attributed to bear positions by market professionals [178].

An article in the September 14, 1931 edition of the New York Times noted that [176]:

WEDNESDAY, SEPTEMBER 2, 1931				
NYSE Volume: 963,395 shares				
Company	Last	Change	%YTD	Dividend
Agricultural Equipment				
Case (J.I.) & Co.	$58^1/_8$	$-4^7/_8$	-35.0%	6
International Harvester	$37^1/_2$	$-\ ^1/_2$	-25.0%	2.50
Autos				
Auburn Auto	134	$-3^1/_2$	$+26.1\%$	4 +8% stk
General Motors	$35^7/_8$	$-\ ^1/_2$	$+1.4\%$	3
Foods				
Coca-Cola	$145^1/_4$	$-\ ^1/_4$	-0.5%	7.75†
General Foods	50	$-\ ^3/_4$	$+2.0\%$	3
Hershey Chocolate	$96^7/_8$	$-1^3/_4$	$+10.1\%$	5
National Biscuit	$57^5/_8$	$-\ ^1/_2$	-25.8%	2.80
Mining				
Anaconda Copper	24	$-\ ^1/_2$	-20.0%	1.50
Colorado Fuel & Iron	13	-1	-39.5%	0
Kennecott Copper	$16^3/_4$	$-\ ^3/_8$	-28.0%	1
Railroads				
New York Central	$67^1/_4$	$-3^3/_4$	-41.3%	6
Pennsylvania R.R.	$37^5/_8$	$-2^3/_8$	-33.1%	3
Southern Pacific	71	$-2^3/_4$	-24.3%	6
Southern Railway	24	$-\ ^1/_2$	-52.7%	6
Union Pacific	139	$-3^1/_2$	-22.8%	10
Retail				
Safeway Stores	63	$-2^5/_8$	$+54.1\%$	5
Sears Roebuck	56	$-\ ^1/_4$	$+24.1\%$	2.50
Woolworth	69	$-\ ^3/_4$	$+24.3\%$	2.40
Steel				
Bethlehem Steel	$38^7/_8$	-1	-23.0%	2
U.S. Steel	$86^1/_8$	$-1^7/_8$	-38.1%	4
Utilities				
Public Service, N. J.	$79^1/_2$	$-1^1/_8$	$+6.7\%$	3.40
Southern Cal. Edison	$43^1/_4$	$-\ ^1/_8$	-6.0%	2
Other Industries				
American Tobacco, B	$109^7/_8$	$-1^1/_8$	$+3.5\%$	6†
General Electric	$40^1/_4$	$-\ ^5/_8$	-7.7%	1.60
Radio Corporation	$19^5/_8$	$-\ ^5/_8$	$+63.5\%$	0
Standard Oil of N. J.	$39^5/_8$	$-\ ^3/_4$	-15.9%	2†
United Aircraft & Tr	$27^1/_8$	$-1^1/_8$	$+13.0\%$	0
† – includes extra dividend				

Table 10.1: Selected stock prices at market close, September 2, 1931 [166]

THURSDAY, SEPTEMBER 3, 1931				
NYSE Volume: 2,131,510 shares				
Company	Last	Change	%YTD	Dividend
Agricultural Equipment				
Case (J.I.) & Co.	$48^1/_2$	$-9^5/_8$	-45.7%	0	
International Harvester	$36^1/_2$	-1	-27.0%	2.50	
Autos				
Auburn Auto	130	-4	$+22.4\%$	4	$+8\%$ stk
General Motors	$34^1/_4$	$-1^5/_8$	-3.2%	3	
Foods				
Coca-Cola	$141^5/_8$	$-3^5/_8$	-3.0%	7.75†
General Foods	49	-1	$+0.0\%$	3
Hershey Chocolate	$96^1/_2$	$-\ ^3/_8$	$+9.7\%$	5
National Biscuit	56	$-1^5/_8$	-27.9%	2.80
Mining				
Anaconda Copper	$23^3/_8$	$-\ ^5/_8$	-22.1%	1.50
Colorado Fuel & Iron	$13^1/_2$	$+\ ^1/_2$	-37.2%	0
Kennecott Copper	$16^5/_8$	$-\ ^1/_8$	-28.5%	1
Railroads				
New York Central	$65^7/_8$	$-1^3/_8$	-42.5%	6
Pennsylvania R.R.	37	$-\ ^5/_8$	-34.2%	3
Southern Pacific	$70^1/_2$	$-\ ^1/_2$	-24.8%	6
Southern Railway	$22^1/_2$	$-1^1/_2$	-55.7%	6
Union Pacific	$135^1/_2$	$-3^1/_2$	-24.7%	10
Retail				
Safeway Stores	$61^5/_8$	$-1^3/_8$	$+50.8\%$	5
Sears Roebuck	$54^1/_2$	$-1^1/_2$	$+20.8\%$	2.50
Woolworth	$67^1/_4$	$-1^3/_4$	$+21.2\%$	2.40
Steel				
Bethlehem Steel	37	$-1^7/_8$	-26.7%	2
U.S. Steel	$83^1/_4$	$-2^7/_8$	-40.2%	4
Utilities				
Public Service, N. J.	78	$-1^1/_2$	$+4.7\%$	3.40
Southern Cal. Edison	$42^3/_4$	$-\ ^1/_2$	-7.1%	2
Other Industries				
American Tobacco, B	$108^3/_4$	$-1^1/_8$	$+2.5\%$	6†
General Electric	$39^5/_8$	$-\ ^5/_8$	-9.2%	1.60
Radio Corporation	$18^5/_8$	-1	$+55.2\%$	0
Standard Oil of N. J.	$39^3/_8$	$-\ ^1/_4$	-16.4%	2†
United Aircraft & Tr	$26^1/_8$	-1	$+8.9\%$	0
† – includes extra dividend				

Table 10.2: Selected stock prices at market close, September 3, 1931 [169]

"The banking community has generally rejected the theory that economic recovery can be promoted through expansion of credit and of money facilities. Most of them point out that reduction in money rates on some markets even below 1 per cent have not been able to revive business ...."

Yet another sharp decline was recorded on Friday, September 18, with the Dow Jones down 6.68 to 115.08 and 2,905,550 shares traded (Table 10.3). Sketchy reports of more problems from London on sterling exchange were noted [179,180]. The concern became more acute the next day when reports showed that the £80,000,000 credit of August 28 had been nearly used up. Prices on the London stock exchange crashed. The sterling exchange rate, which had fallen $1/8$ cents on Friday, plunged $1 5/16$ cents midday and closed down $15/16$ cents at $4.84$1/2$ [183]. The Dow Jones closed down 3.34 at 111.74.

10.2   Bond Market Crash

The crash in the bond markets was even more spectacular. Whereas bond prices had been somewhat volatile but fairly firm during the 1929 crash, they crashed along with stocks throughout September (Figure 10.1). The New York Times index of 40 domestic bonds fell nearly continuously from 81.15 on September 1 to 75.61 on September 19 – a day on which the index lost 1.14 points (Table 10.4). The New York Times index of 10 high-grade foreign bonds (Figure 10.2) similarly tumbled from 105.00 on September 1 to 99.41 on September 19. The index lost 1.46 points on September 18 and 1.65 points on September 19 alone [184]. Credit was evaporating, taking the economy with it.

10.3   End of the British Gold Standard – September 20, 1931

On Sunday, September 20, 1931, the British government abruptly announced that redemption of pounds for gold, per the 1925 Gold Standard Act, would be suspended [188]. The necessary legislation would be passed by Parliament and signed by the King the next day, with the House of Lords meeting in a rare emergency session [186]. Gold reserves at the Bank

FRIDAY, SEPTEMBER 18, 1931				
NYSE Volume: 2,905,550 shares				
Company	Last	Change	%YTD	Dividend
Agricultural Equipment				
Case (J.I.) & Co.	$44^1/_4$	$-2^3/_4$	−50.5%	0
International Harvester	29	$+ ^1/_8$	−42.0%	2.50
Autos				
Auburn Auto	117	$-6^3/_4$	+10.1%	4 +8% stk
General Motors	30	$-2^1/_8$	−15.2%	3
Foods				
Coca-Cola	$129^3/_8$	$-3^5/_8$	−11.4%	7.75†
General Foods	$43^7/_8$	$-1^5/_8$	−10.5%	3
Hershey Chocolate	$84^1/_2$	$-3^1/_2$	−4.0%	5
National Biscuit	43	$-2^5/_8$	−44.6%	2.80
Mining				
Anaconda Copper	$17^1/_4$	$-1^5/_8$	−42.5%	1.50
Colorado Fuel & Iron	$10^1/_2$	$- ^7/_8$	−51.2%	0
Kennecott Copper	13	−1	−44.1%	1
Railroads				
New York Central	$59^1/_8$	$-3^3/_4$	−48.4%	4
Pennsylvania R.R.	32	$-1^1/_4$	−43.1%	3
Southern Pacific	$59^3/_4$	$-3^3/_4$	−36.3%	6
Southern Railway	$18^1/_8$	$-1^3/_4$	−64.3%	6
Union Pacific	$113^1/_4$	$-9^3/_4$	−37.1%	10
Retail				
Safeway Stores	$52^3/_4$	$-2^1/_2$	+29.1%	5
Sears Roebuck	$47^1/_4$	$-2^3/_4$	+4.7%	2.50
Woolworth	$58^1/_2$	$-3^1/_2$	+5.4%	2.40
Steel				
Bethlehem Steel	$34^1/_8$	$-1^7/_8$	−32.4%	2
U.S. Steel	$77^1/_2$	$-3^1/_2$	−44.3%	4
Utilities				
Public Service, N. J.	$69^1/_4$	$-2^1/_4$	−7.0%	3.40
Southern Cal. Edison	$37^1/_4$	$-1^1/_4$	−19.0%	2
Other Industries				
American Tobacco, B	$97^5/_8$	$-6^1/_2$	−8.0%	6†
General Electric	$32^3/_4$	$-1^3/_4$	−24.9%	1.60
Radio Corporation	15	$-1^1/_4$	+25.0%	0
Standard Oil of N. J.	$33^5/_8$	$-1^1/_2$	−28.6%	2†
United Aircraft & Tr	$19^5/_8$	$-1^7/_8$	−18.2%	0
† – includes extra dividend				

Table 10.3: Selected stock prices at market close, September 18, 1931 [181]

Figure 10.1: NY Times domestic bond index, 1929 - 1932 [246]

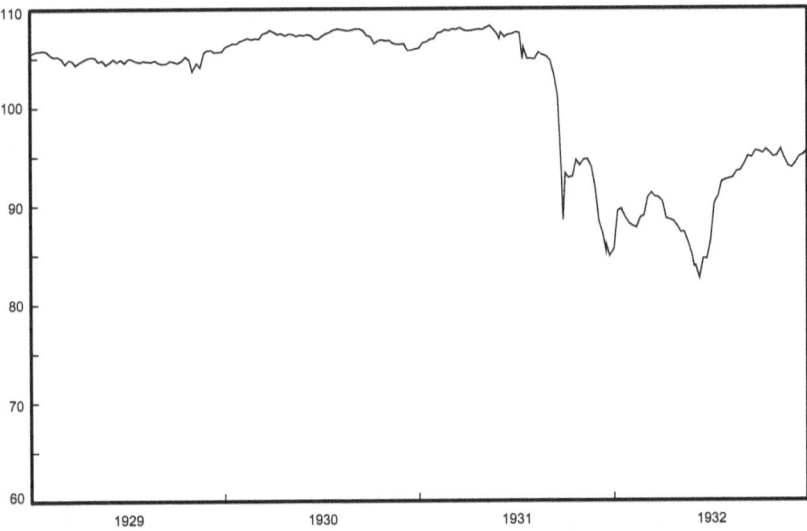

Figure 10.2: NY Times foreign bond index, 1929 - 1932 [246]

SATURDAY, SEPTEMBER 19, 1931				
Company/Issue	Bond Price	Change	Current Yield	Yield to Maturity
Railroads				
New York Central 5s2013	96	$-\frac{1}{4}$	5.2%	5.2%
Pennsylvania R.R. $4\frac{1}{2}$s1970	$80\frac{3}{4}$	$-2\frac{1}{4}$	5.6%	5.7%
Southern Pacific $4\frac{1}{2}$s1968	79	-1	5.7%	5.9%
Southern Railway 4s1956	$59\frac{3}{4}$	-1	6.7%	7.6%
Union Pacific 4s1968	91	$+\frac{1}{8}$	4.4%	4.5%
Utilities				
Public Service E&G $4\frac{1}{2}$s1970	102	$-2\frac{1}{2}$	4.4%	4.4%
Other Industries				
Bethlehem Steel 5s1936	100	$-$	5.0%	5.0%
General Motors 6s1937	$103\frac{1}{8}$	$-\frac{1}{8}$	5.8%	5.4%
Standard Oil of N.J. 5s1946	$103\frac{1}{4}$	$-\frac{1}{2}$	4.8%	4.7%

Table 10.4: Selected bond prices at market close, September 19, 1931 [185]

of England had dwindled to £130,000,000 – the same amount as the credits that had been granted by the U.S. and France in the previous month [191]. The suspension was said to be "temporary;" [187] however, it was never resumed. 233 years of currency stability (with a few lapses) had come to an end [32, p. 29-30].

The London Times criticized the United States and France harshly, saying that "The gold standard game ... cannot be played on the new rules practised since the war by France and the United States" – meaning that the two countries had failed to increase their supply of money to reflect gold inflows. The merits of this criticism are dubious regarding the United States, which had in fact had significant monetary inflation since 1921 that was only partially reversed starting in 1929. It is true that France did not expand its money supply in the same proportion as its gold holdings grew, but if the French government made a commitment to redeem francs for gold at a fixed rate, can they be faulted for amassing the gold needed to keep their promise? The London Times did accurately state that "prohibitive tariffs keep out goods, and unless the creditor nations relend the credits due to them the debtor nations must pay gold to the extent of their resources and then default." [186]

Aside from the inherent instability of fractional reserve banking, inflation during World War I was the initial source of the monetary disruption [255, pp. 101-104]. Also, Great Britain, while making a noble effort to repay her war creditors in full, did not impose the necessary austerity policies of allowing price deflation and wage cuts that would have fulfilled such a commitment. Instead, Great Britain had begun a "most expensive experiment in socialism" with unemployment insurance that provided a comparatively high standard of living for those with no work [186]. The balancing of the budget in September via a 10% cut to the unemployment dole and a 25% increase in taxes was insufficient (and probably too late) to save the pound[1] [5, p. 116].

It is debatable how much of a factor that the 1925 decision to restore the pound at pre-war gold parity played in the 1931 devaluation. Had the pound been formally devalued in 1925 when gold payments were resumed, it certainly would have been easier to defend the pound in 1931. However, the international trade barriers and growing statism of the 1920s and 1930s would still have collapsed economic growth and the value of outstanding debt. These factors were eroding the value of most currencies around the world – including the U.S. dollar – relative to gold. The 30% drop in the pound's value from parity by December of 1931 indicates that significant factors other the 1925 decision were present. (Besides the credit collapse, the conversion of the pound from a gold-backed to a fiat currency reduced its desirability and hence its value [253, p. 105].) Although the pound devaluation crisis might have come a little later and been slightly less severe, reducing the gold equivalent of the pound in 1925 by 10% would probably have led to more or less the same outcome seven years later anyway.

Some authors have harshly criticized the manner in which Britain abandoned the gold standard [254, p. 259-260], [253, pp. 93-96], [208]. They noted that the British discount rate never exceeded $4\frac{1}{2}$% throughout 1931 until *after* the gold standard was dropped, whereas in past financial crises, the Bank of England had raised the discount rate to 10%. Rothbard termed the British action "shabby," writing that "Aided by France instead of the reverse, much stronger financially than Germany or Austria, England cynically repudiated its obligations without a struggle, while Germany and Austria had at least fought frantically to save themselves." Robbins makes similar comments about the hypocrisy of Britain's cheap money policy, noting that the gold standard might have been beyond salvation by this time,

---

[1]The additional weight on the economy added by the tax increases may well have accelerated the pound's slide [32, p. 220].

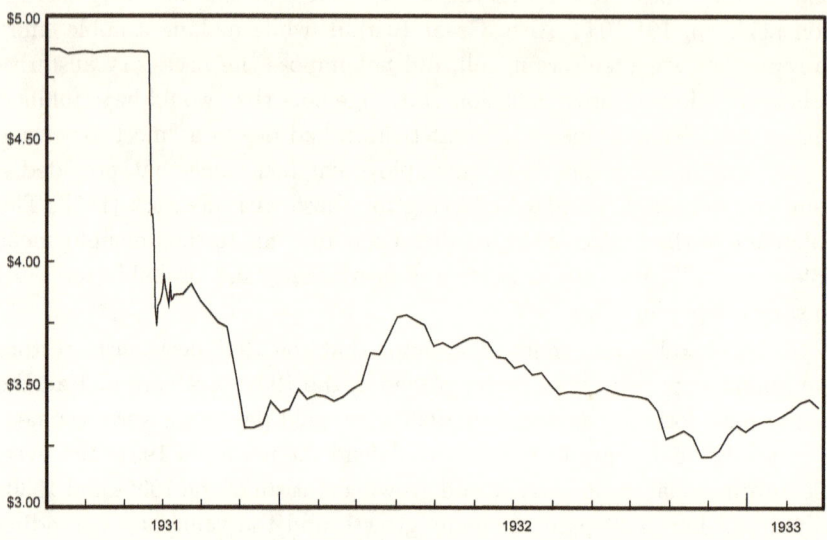

Figure 10.3: Weekly sterling exchange rate, 1931 - 1932 [248]

but an increase of the bank rate at least offered a chance by signaling to the world that there was a commitment to maintaining the pound's value. Benjamin M. Anderson, Jr., economist of Chase National Bank, likewise wrote that an increase in the discount rate to 8% or 9% in August would have saved the gold standard [208].

The pound fell sharply to $3.70 in exchange quotations the next day before closing at $4.19 – a one-day drop of 14%. The pound continued to fluctuate enormously throughout the week as traders sought its true value (Figure 10.3), settling around $3.82 at the end of the week (a 21.5% drop in value from parity).

The British pound devaluation had worldwide impacts, as roughly 60% of the world's business was transacted in pounds [5, p. 119], [189]. The devaluation immediately inflicted large losses on all holders of pounds. Holland, Sweden, and Switzerland, as creditors of pound-denominated debts, were hardest hit, while pound debtors, such as Germany and Austria, obtained some relief [189].

10.4   International Collapse of the Gold Standard

The British devaluation started runs on gold reserves around the world as currency holders sought to preserve the value of their holdings. The United States was not spared – U.S. gold reserves, which touched $5,000,000,000 in mid-September, dropped 5% in the last ten days of the month as the credit of the dollar was doubted for the first time.

On September 21, the day after the British announcement, Denmark suspended gold exports. The Danish krone immediately dropped 7% on foreign exchange markets and was down as much as 20% from parity later in the week [193]. Austria instituted foreign exchange controls on September 23. Similar to Germany, these controls were in effect an abandonment of the gold standard [192].

One week after Britain's announcement, Sweden, Norway, and Egypt all suspended gold redemptions. They had all suffered serious runs on their gold reserves. Sweden had lost 100,000,000 kroner of foreign exchange reserves in one week. Bankers in New York and Paris believed that a proposed credit of about 300,000,000 kroner ($75,000,000) credit would have been futile in view of the worldwide panic. Like Britain, Sweden had lent considerable money to Germany [193].

The exchange rate volatility that developed (Figure 10.4) further hampered foreign trade due to the high risks of loss from currency fluctuations [253, pp. 116-119], particularly in a world that was unaccustomed to such risks. The foreign currency devaluations also pushed U.S. prices further down, as foreigners now simply had less money (in terms of dollars) to offer for purchasing U.S. goods.

10.5   Reaction in U.S. Markets

The initial reaction of the stock market to the devaluation news was remarkably calm. Whereas the London and Berlin stock exchanges were closed on Monday, September 21 [188, 190], the New York Stock Exchange remained open and prices changed relatively little (the Dow closed down just 0.91 at 110.83). After a bump upward to 115.99 on Wednesday, September 23, stock prices resumed their downward slide, with the Dow finishing the month at 96.61 (Table 10.5). The monthly decline of 30.7% remains the

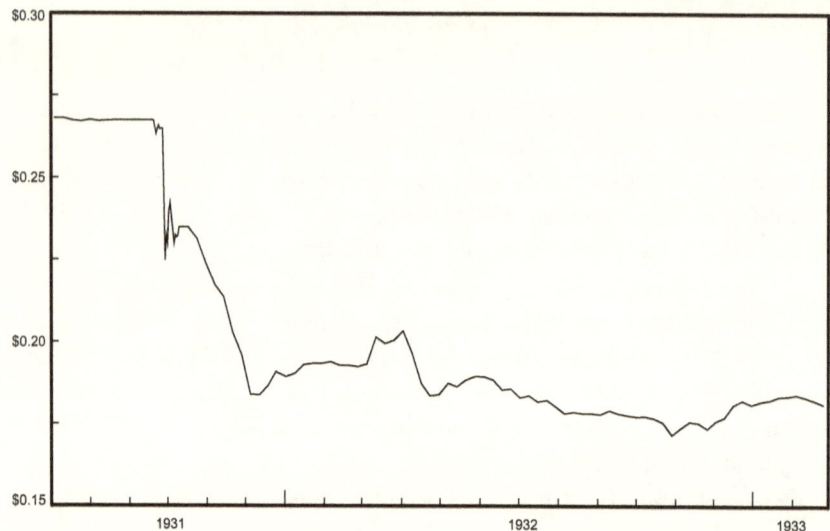

Figure 10.4: Weekly Swedish krona exchange rate, 1931 - 1932 [248]

worst on record.

Domestic bonds behaved similarly, with the NY Times domestic bond index initially falling 1.06 points to 74.55 on September 21, rallying 1.87 points to 76.09 on September 23, and then sliding for the remainder of the month to 72.77 on September 30. The decline in the domestic bond index for the month was 10.0%.

Foreign bonds crashed on the day after the devaluation announcement, with the NY Times foreign bond index falling 3.90 points to 95.51. The index recovered 1.80 points over the next two days but then fell steeply, reaching 88.54 after a 4.70-point loss on September 28. A rebound on the last two days of the month brought the index to 90.67 at the close of September – a loss of 13.5% for the month.

At this point, the depression had truly become Great.

WEDNESDAY, SEPTEMBER 30, 1931				
Company	Stock Price	%YTD	Annual Dividend Rate	Dividend Yield
Agricultural Equipment				
Case (J.I.) & Co.	$38^1/_4$	−57.2%	0	0.0%
International Harvester	$25^7/_8$	−48.2%	2.50	9.7%
Autos				
Auburn Auto	$95^3/_4$	−9.9%	4 +8% stk	4.2%
General Motors	$23^5/_8$	−33.2%	3	12.7%
Foods				
Coca-Cola	$103^3/_4$	−28.9%	7.75†	7.5%
General Foods	35	−28.6%	3	8.6%
Hershey Chocolate	75	−14.8%	5	6.7%
National Biscuit	41	−47.2%	2.80	6.8%
Mining				
Anaconda Copper	15	−50.0%	0	0.0%
Colorado Fuel & Iron	$8^3/_8$	−61.0%	0	0.0%
Kennecott Copper	$11^3/_4$	−49.5%	1	8.5%
Railroads				
New York Central	$62^1/_2$	−45.4%	4	6.4%
Pennsylvania R.R.	$32^1/_4$	−42.7%	3	9.3%
Southern Pacific	$55^1/_8$	−41.2%	6	10.9%
Southern Railway	19	−62.6%	6	31.6%
Union Pacific	114	−36.7%	10	8.8%
Retail				
Safeway Stores	$43^1/_8$	+5.5%	5	11.6%
Sears Roebuck	$34^5/_8$	−23.3%	2.50	7.2%
Woolworth	$48^1/_2$	−12.6%	2.40	4.9%
Steel				
Bethlehem Steel	$28^3/_4$	−43.1%	2	7.0%
U.S. Steel	$71^3/_8$	−48.7%	4	5.6%
Utilities				
Public Service, N. J.	$56^1/_8$	−24.7%	3.40	6.1%
Southern Cal. Edison	$31^3/_4$	−31.0%	2	6.3%
Other Industries				
American Tobacco, B	$85^1/_8$	−19.8%	6†	7.0%
General Electric	$27^3/_8$	−37.2%	1.60	5.8%
Radio Corporation	$12^1/_2$	+4.2%	0	0.0%
Standard Oil of N. J.	$29^5/_8$	−37.1%	2†	6.8%
United Aircraft & Tr	$15^1/_8$	−37.0%	0	0.0%
† − includes extra dividend				

Table 10.5: Selected stock prices at market close, September 30, 1931 [196]

Chapter 11

Oct.-Dec. 1931: The Aftermath

Following the British devaluation crisis of September, paper currencies, including the dollar, were no longer trusted in international trade [5, p. 119, 150, 251]. A run began on U.S. gold reserves as foreign nations, especially France, exchanged dollars for gold. The Federal Reserve reacted to the gold drain by raising the discount rate two percentage points in just 8 days – the most rapid increase in the history of the Federal Reserve System [21, p. 317]. The gold supply stabilized a couple of weeks after this action. (Hoover would later state that the U.S. would have been forced off the gold standard if the drain had continued into mid-November [228], [229].)

With monetary austerity imposed by the collapse of credit and the associated raising of rates to protect the gold standard, it is no surprise that the economy sank precipitously as credit was reduced. The full impact of the growing international trade barriers on the economy could no longer be postponed by cheap credit. Unemployment increased to unprecedented levels in U.S. history; for the year, the average unemployment rate was 15.9% [41, p. 103]. The contraction and steep deflation were undeniably brutal as consumption was forcibly reduced to match the exchange value of production and the economy finally started liquidating its weaknesses to a significant extent. Unfortunately, officials still looked for a return to cheap credit in a misguided effort at recovery. True recovery required, preferably, a lowering of the international trade walls. Failing that, recovery was incumbent on a liquidation of export-driven capital, which was now of diminished value. While leaving the country markedly poorer than it was in the 1920s, such liquidation would at least have provided a floor from which the economy could truly grow again.

11.1   Gold

The gold drain that began in the latter part of September continued into October. $725,000,000 of gold flowed out in the six week period from the middle of September to the end of October – a 14% drop [21, p. 316]. The stock market continued its slide as October began, with the Dow Jones average dropping 4.11 points to 92.77 on Saturday, October 3 and another 6.29 points (6.8%) on Monday, October 5 (Tables 11.1 and 11.2). The next day, the market rallied strongly, with the Dow up 12.86 (14.9%) to 99.34 (Tables 11.3 and 11.4). President Hoover announced his plan for a private national credit corporation that day, although analysts generally attributed the rally to a rebound from an oversold condition [199], [200]. The Dow had, after all, fallen 38.3% since September 1.

On October 8, the New York Federal Reserve Bank raised the discount rate from $1\frac{1}{2}$% to $2\frac{1}{2}$%. Interestingly, the stock market rallied strongly again (the Dow was up 8.47 (8.7%) to 105.79), with bank stocks leading the way. The Fed stated publicly that the $1\frac{1}{2}$% discount rate (the lowest central bank rate in recorded world history up to that time) had failed to meet its objectives and that it desired a restoration of more normal conditions in the money markets [203]. Although the Fed emphatically stated that the rate hike had nothing to do with the gold outflow (indeed, they stated that the outflow was desirable), internal discussions by the bank's board of directors indicate the opposite [21, pp. 380-382]. With gold still pouring out, the N.Y. Fed discount rate was raised again on October 15 from $2\frac{1}{2}$% to $3\frac{1}{2}$%. With this hike, the rate was now 1% higher than the discount rate of the Bank of France. Analysts noted that the cheap money policy had in fact become counterproductive [204].

Reporters stated that the rate hikes were instituted to combat "hoarding." Currency in circulation in the U.S. was $5.431 billion, 21% higher than one year earlier [203]. Hoarding, however, is in fact a rational and logical course of action during times of uncertainty. Hoarding – waiting for clarity – is often the most profitable course of action during times of high risk, since investment decisions can be postponed [15]. Investors desire stable economic signals to determine appropriate investment alloca-

MONDAY, OCTOBER 5, 1931 NYSE Volume: 3,191,670 shares					
Company	Last	Change	%YTD	Dividend	
Agricultural Equipment					
Case (J.I.) & Co.	$33^5/_8$	$-4^1/_2$	-62.4%	0	
International Harvester	$23^1/_2$	$-1^1/_2$	-53.0%	2.50	
Autos					
Auburn Auto	$84^1/_2$	-10	-20.5%	4	+8% stk
General Motors	$22^1/_2$	$-\,^5/_8$	-36.4%	3	
Foods					
Coca-Cola	$97^3/_4$	$-8^1/_8$	-33.0%	7.75†	
General Foods	$30^5/_8$	-3	-37.5%	3	
Hershey Chocolate	$71^5/_8$	$-1^3/_8$	-18.6%	5	
National Biscuit	$38^3/_4$	$-1^3/_8$	-50.1%	2.80	
Mining					
Anaconda Copper	13	$-1^3/_4$	-56.7%	0	
Colorado Fuel & Iron	$8^1/_2$	$-\,^1/_8$	-60.5%	0	
Kennecott Copper	$10^1/_4$	-1	-55.9%	1	
Railroads					
New York Central	50	$-5^1/_8$	-56.3%	4	
Pennsylvania R.R.	$29^7/_8$	$-1^3/_4$	-46.9%	3	
Southern Pacific	$45^1/_8$	$-5^5/_8$	-51.9%	6	
Southern Railway	15	$-1^3/_4$	-70.4%	6	
Union Pacific	$98^1/_4$	$-6^7/_8$	-45.4%	10	
Retail					
Safeway Stores	$40^1/_8$	$-3^5/_8$	-1.8%	5	
Sears Roebuck	31	$-1^1/_4$	-31.3%	2.50	
Woolworth	$43^3/_8$	$-3^5/_8$	-21.8%	2.40	
Steel					
Bethlehem Steel	$25^1/_8$	-1	-50.2%	2	
U.S. Steel	$62^1/_4$	$-6^1/_4$	-55.3%	4	
Utilities					
Public Service, N. J.	$52^1/_2$	$-4^1/_4$	-29.5%	3.40	
Southern Cal. Edison	$28^3/_8$	$-1^5/_8$	-38.3%	2	
Other Industries					
American Tobacco, B	$75^1/_8$	-3	-29.2%	6†	
General Electric	$24^3/_4$	$-1^1/_4$	-43.3%	1.60	
Radio Corporation	$10^7/_8$	$-1^1/_4$	-9.4%	0	
Standard Oil of N. J.	$28^3/_8$	$-\,^3/_4$	-39.8%	2†	
United Aircraft & Tr	$12^1/_4$	$-1^5/_8$	-49.0%	0	
† – includes extra dividend					

Table 11.1: Selected stock prices at market close, October 5, 1931 [197]

MONDAY, OCTOBER 5, 1931				
Company/Issue	Bond Price	Change	Current Yield	Yield to Maturity
Railroads				
New York Central 5s2013	89	$-1\frac{1}{2}$	5.6%	5.6%
Pennsylvania R.R. $4\frac{1}{2}$s1970	$72\frac{1}{2}$	-3	6.2%	6.4%
Southern Pacific $4\frac{1}{2}$s1968	$72\frac{1}{4}$	$-\frac{3}{8}$	6.2%	6.5%
Southern Railway 4s1956	$51\frac{3}{4}$	$-5\frac{1}{4}$	7.7%	8.8%
Union Pacific 4s1968	80	-2	5.0%	5.2%
Utilities				
Public Service E&G $4\frac{1}{2}$s1970	100	$-\frac{1}{4}$	4.5%	4.5%
Other Industries				
Bethlehem Steel 5s1936	99	$+\frac{1}{2}$	5.1%	5.2%
General Motors 6s1937	$99\frac{1}{4}$	$-\frac{1}{4}$	6.0%	6.2%
Standard Oil of N.J. 5s1946	$100\frac{1}{2}$	$-\frac{1}{2}$	5.0%	5.0%

Table 11.2: Selected bond prices at market close, October 5, 1931 [198]

tion. Moreover, accumulation of large hoards generates a rapid economic recovery when business conditions become favorable. In a more predictable situation, those hoards can be put to the best economic uses.

11.2   Bank Runs

With deteriorated business conditions, bank failures and suspensions, which spiked to a high of $471,380,000 of deposits in October, remained very high through the end of the year. Bank runs did not subside until the start of 1932, when they dropped significantly (Figures 5.10 and 5.11). For the year, 2,293 banks were suspended, with $1.69 billion of deposits [29].

As noted above, on October 6 President Hoover announced a plan to form what would become the National Credit Corporation (NCC). The NCC was a private banker consortium that would make loans to businesses in trouble and would be funded by $500,000,000 from the country's top banks. Another $1,000,000,000 would be borrowed from the Federal Reserve. The NCC was to be temporary, but it was intended as a prelude to the Reconstruction Finance Corporation (RFC) that would be formed early the following year [254, pp. 274-276].

Aided by a spike in agricultural prices [5, p. 124], the stock market re-

TUESDAY, OCTOBER 6, 1931 NYSE Volume: 4,300,574 shares					
Company	Last	Change	%YTD	Dividend	
Agricultural Equipment					
Case (J.I.) & Co.	41³/₈	+7³/₄	−53.7%	0	
International Harvester	25¹/₄	+1³/₄	−49.5%	2.50	
Autos					
Auburn Auto	99	+14¹/₂	−6.8%	4	+8% stk
General Motors	25	+2¹/₂	−29.3%	3	
Foods					
Coca-Cola	105¹/₄	+7¹/₂	−27.9%	7.75†	
General Foods	35	+4³/₈	−28.6%	3	
Hershey Chocolate	75	+3³/₈	−14.8%	5	
National Biscuit	43¹/₂	+4³/₄	−44.0%	2.80	
Mining					
Anaconda Copper	14¹/₂	+1¹/₂	−51.7%	0	
Colorado Fuel & Iron	10	+1¹/₂	−53.5%	0	
Kennecott Copper	12	+1³/₄	−48.4%	1	
Railroads					
New York Central	57¹/₂	+7¹/₂	−49.8%	4	
Pennsylvania R.R.	33⁵/₈	+3³/₄	−40.2%	3	
Southern Pacific	50	+4⁷/₈	−46.7%	6	
Southern Railway	17⁷/₈	+2⁷/₈	−64.8%	6	
Union Pacific	110	+11³/₄	−38.9%	10	
Retail					
Safeway Stores	46	+5⁷/₈	+12.5%	5	
Sears Roebuck	35³/₄	+4³/₄	−20.8%	2.50	
Woolworth	49³/₈	+6	−11.0%	2.40	
Steel					
Bethlehem Steel	29⁵/₈	+4¹/₂	−41.3%	2	
U.S. Steel	71¹/₈	+8⁷/₈	−48.9%	4	
Utilities					
Public Service, N. J.	60³/₄	+8¹/₄	−18.5%	3.40	
Southern Cal. Edison	31¹/₄	+2⁷/₈	−32.1%	2	
Other Industries					
American Tobacco, B	83¹/₂	+8³/₈	−21.3%	6†	
General Electric	28³/₈	+3⁵/₈	−35.0%	1.60	
Radio Corporation	13	+2¹/₈	+8.3%	0	
Standard Oil of N. J.	31³/₄	+3³/₈	−32.6%	2†	
United Aircraft & Tr	15¹/₈	+2⁷/₈	−37.0%	0	
† – includes extra dividend					

Table 11.3: Selected stock prices at market close, October 6, 1931 [201]

TUESDAY, OCTOBER 6, 1931				
Company/Issue	Bond Price	Change	Current Yield	Yield to Maturity
Railroads				
New York Central 5s2013	91	+2	5.5%	5.5%
Pennsylvania R.R. 4$\frac{1}{2}$s1970	76	+3$\frac{1}{2}$	5.9%	6.1%
Southern Pacific 4$\frac{1}{2}$s1968	74	+1$\frac{3}{4}$	6.1%	6.3%
Southern Railway 4s1956	54$\frac{1}{2}$	+2$\frac{3}{4}$	7.3%	8.4%
Union Pacific 4s1968	81$\frac{1}{2}$	+1$\frac{1}{2}$	4.9%	5.1%
Utilities				
Public Service E&G 4$\frac{1}{2}$s1970	101$\frac{1}{4}$	+1$\frac{1}{4}$	4.4%	4.4%
Other Industries				
Bethlehem Steel 5s1936	99	–	5.1%	5.2%
General Motors 6s1937	99$\frac{1}{4}$	–	6.0%	6.2%
Standard Oil of N.J. 5s1946	101$\frac{3}{4}$	+1$\frac{1}{4}$	4.9%	4.8%

Table 11.4: Selected bond prices at market close, October 6, 1931 [202]

bound continued into mid-November, with the Dow Jones average reaching 116.79 on November 9 (Tables 11.5 and 11.6). The rally fizzled after that, however, and the stock market sank steadily through the rest of the year, hitting its lowest levels for 1931 just before the end of the year (73.84 on December 28) (Tables 11.7 and 11.8).

11.3   England

A few riots, many of which were abetted by Communists, came in response to the September cuts to the unemployment dole [195], but the austerity measures, and a 6% discount rate, acted to contain the extent of the currency collapse. The pound fluctuated around $3.85 through most of October and then sank below $3.50 at the start of December, but it started to recover afterward. Prices rose 10% in the last few months of the year even with continued high unemployment. (The rapidly deepening worldwide depression, influenced by the very instability of the pound's value, offset much of the price increase that would otherwise have been expected from a 30% currency devaluation [253, pp. 104-105, 114-117].) Exports rebounded as a result of the drop in prices relative to gold [5, p. 123]. At the end of October, Britain was able to repay $100,000,000 of the $650,000,000 in emergency

	Stock		Annual	Dividend
Company	Price	%YTD	Dividend Rate	Yield
MONDAY, NOVEMBER 9, 1931				
Agricultural Equipment				
Case (J.I.) & Co.	55	−38.5%	0	0.0%
International Harvester	35³/₄	−28.5%	2.50	7.0%
Autos				
Auburn Auto	137¹/₂	+29.4%	4 +8% stk	2.9%
General Motors	29³/₄	−15.9%	3	10.1%
Foods				
Coca-Cola	126	−13.7%	8†	6.3%
General Foods	40¹/₂	−17.3%	3	7.4%
National Biscuit	53³/₄	−30.8%	2.80	5.2%
Mining				
Anaconda Copper	19	−36.7%	0	0.0%
Colorado Fuel & Iron	14	−34.9%	0	0.0%
Kennecott Copper	17¹/₈	−26.3%	1	5.8%
Railroads				
New York Central	53¹/₄	−53.5%	4	7.5%
Pennsylvania R.R.	33	−41.3%	2	6.1%
Southern Pacific	53¹/₂	−42.9%	6	11.2%
Southern Railway	17¹/₂	−65.5%	6	34.3%
Union Pacific	112	−37.8%	10	8.9%
Retail				
Safeway Stores	53¹/₂	+30.9%	5	9.3%
Sears Roebuck	46⁷/₈	+3.9%	2.50	5.3%
Woolworth	55¹/₂	+0.0%	4.40†	7.9%
Steel				
Bethlehem Steel	32³/₄	−35.1%	2	6.1%
U.S. Steel	73⁷/₈	−46.9%	4	5.4%
Utilities				
Public Service, N. J.	69¹/₂	−6.7%	3.40	4.9%
Southern Cal. Edison	38	−17.4%	2	5.3%
Other Industries				
American Tobacco, B	97¹/₂	−8.1%	6†	6.2%
General Electric	34¹/₂	−20.9%	1.60	4.6%
Radio Corporation	13³/₄	+14.6%	0	0.0%
Standard Oil of N. J.	37¹/₈	−21.2%	2†	5.4%
United Aircraft & Tr	18³/₈	−23.4%	0	0.0%
† – includes extra dividend				

Table 11.5: Selected stock prices at market close, November 9, 1931 [206]

Monday, November 9, 1931			
Company/Issue	Bond Price	Current Yield	Yield to Maturity
Railroads			
New York Central 5s2013	91^1/$_4$	5.5%	5.5%
Pennsylvania R.R. 4^1/$_2$s1970	80^1/$_4$	5.6%	5.8%
Southern Pacific 4^1/$_2$s1968	78^1/$_8$	5.8%	6.0%
Southern Railway 4s1956	60	6.7%	7.6%
Union Pacific 4s1968	82	4.9%	5.1%
Utilities			
Public Service E&G 4^1/$_2$s1970	99^1/$_4$	4.5%	4.5%
Other Industries			
Bethlehem Steel 5s1936	99^1/$_4$	5.0%	5.2%
General Motors 6s1937	102^1/$_4$	5.9%	5.6%
Standard Oil of N.J. 5s1946	102	4.9%	4.8%

Table 11.6: Selected bond prices at market close, November 9, 1931 [207]

credits that had been extended by the U.S. and France in August [205].
(These credits, of course, were not affected by the pound devaluation.) By
April 1, 1932, $550,000,000 had been repaid [5, p. 152], [221]. Britons who
traveled abroad discovered how much poorer they suddenly were as a result of the devaluation [253, p. 106], but a cut in domestic consumption
was needed to restore balance with the economy's production.

11.4 Japan

Japan banned gold exports on December 13 [210] and suspended gold redemptions by the next day [211], [218], adding itself to the growing list of
countries abandoning the gold standard. Exchange quotations for the yen
plummeted from 48.44 cents to 42.94 cents on the day before the official
announcement of the gold embargo [209]. Japan had only recently (January 11, 1930) returned to the gold standard after its suspension during
World War I. The great earthquake of 1923 was a major factor delaying its
restoration [66].

Japan's "warlike operations in Manchuria"[1] combined with the financial

---

[1]Interestingly, Japanese troops seized control of the Manchurian capital city of Mukden on September 19 [182], just one day before Great Britain went off the gold standard.

THURSDAY, DECEMBER 31, 1931				
Company	Stock Price	%YTD	Annual Dividend Rate	Dividend Yield
Agricultural Equipment				
Case (J.I.) & Co.	$40^7/_8$	−54.3%	0	0.0%
International Harvester	24	−52.0%	2.50	10.4%
Autos				
Auburn Auto	131	+23.3%	4 +8% stk	3.1%
General Motors	$22^5/_8$	−36.0%	3	13.3%
Foods				
Coca-Cola	107	−26.7%	8†	7.5%
General Foods	34	−30.6%	3	8.8%
Hershey Chocolate	$80^3/_4$	−8.2%	6	7.4%
National Biscuit	$40^1/_8$	−48.3%	2.80	7.0%
Mining				
Anaconda Copper	$9^7/_8$	−67.1%	0	0.0%
Colorado Fuel & Iron	$7^5/_8$	−64.5%	0	0.0%
Kennecott Copper	$11^1/_4$	−51.6%	0.50	4.4%
Railroads				
New York Central	29	−74.7%	0	0.0%
Pennsylvania R.R.	$18^1/_8$	−67.8%	2	11.0%
Southern Pacific	$27^3/_4$	−70.4%	4	14.4%
Southern Railway	$7^1/_2$	−85.2%	0	0.0%
Union Pacific	71	−60.6%	10	14.1%
Retail				
Safeway Stores	$43^3/_8$	+6.1%	5	11.5%
Sears Roebuck	33	−26.9%	2.50	7.6%
Woolworth	40	−27.9%	4.40†	11.0%
Steel				
Bethlehem Steel	$18^3/_4$	−62.9%	2	10.7%
U.S. Steel	$38^5/_8$	−72.2%	4	10.4%
Utilities				
Public Service, N. J.	$54^1/_4$	−27.2%	3.40	6.3%
Southern Cal. Edison	$31^1/_2$	−31.5%	2	6.3%
Other Industries				
American Tobacco, B	$69^3/_4$	−34.3%	6†	8.6%
General Electric	25	−42.7%	1.60	6.4%
Radio Corporation	$5^1/_2$	−54.2%	0	0.0%
Standard Oil of N. J.	$27^7/_8$	−40.8%	2†	7.2%
United Aircraft & Tr	$11^1/_4$	−53.1%	0	0.0%
† – includes extra dividend				

Table 11.7: Selected stock prices at market close, December 31, 1931 [219]

| Thursday, December 31, 1931 | | | |
Company/Issue	Bond Price	Current Yield	Yield to Maturity
Railroads			
New York Central 5s2013	76	6.6%	6.6%
Pennsylvania R.R. 4¹/₂s1970	65¹/₄	6.9%	7.2%
Southern Pacific 4¹/₂s1968	61⁵/₈	7.3%	7.6%
Southern Railway 4s1956	41¹/₂	9.6%	10.8%
Union Pacific 4s1968	71	5.6%	5.9%
Utilities			
Public Service E&G 4¹/₂s1970	96	4.7%	4.7%
Other Industries			
Bethlehem Steel 5s1936	94	5.3%	6.4%
General Motors 6s1937	97³/₄	6.1%	6.5%
Standard Oil of N.J. 5s1946	100¹/₂	5.0%	5.0%

Table 11.8: Selected bond prices at market close, December 31, 1931 [220]

strain of the depression to spur a flight of foreign capital [211]. International trade barriers were already leading some nations to pursue military solutions to their economic woes [32, p. 226].

11.5   War Debt Resolution

Most people today would probably not be surprised that Congress did not act on the Hoover Moratorium before the December 15 debt installment deadline. With Congress still debating, Hoover assured debtor nations on December 14 that lack of payment would not be construed as default or "subjected to just criticism" [212]. On December 18, the House approved the Moratorium by a 317-100 vote but recorded an objection to debt revision or cancellation. Despite a broadly acclaimed statement from Rep. La Guardia (R-N.Y.) that Hitler would quickly take power if Germany's economy did not obtain some relief – a scenario that would soon become all too real – the debate in the House was testy; a number of representatives bitterly opposed the debt moratorium, with some charging that it was

---

This Japanese action – regarded by some historians as the start of World War II – was not considered by contemporary commentators as a factor in the British monetary decision [186], [208], although some subsequent writers [32, p. 226] note its adverse impact.

solely for the benefit of international bankers. (Some things never change!) Moratorium opponents also criticized the continuing military expenditures of debtor nations that were claiming to be unable to pay their debts [213]. This was a valid concern, but it overlooked the fact that American protective tariffs had prevented debtor nations from supplying goods to pay their debts and disrupted international trade so much that the debt payments now being demanded of debtor nations were in effect overvalued in terms of gold. The hostile attitude toward debt revision by many in Congress prompted the exchange value of sterling to drop $0.10 the same day [214]. The Senate approved the Hoover Moratorium 69-12 on December 22 after similarly rancorous debate [215].

11.6 December Retail

The December Christmas retail season was reported to be about the same as the previous year in volume of sales, but prices were much lower, resulting in a corresponding drop in dollar sales figures. Philadelphia reported a "strong turnover." Minneapolis volume was down slightly, and dollar sales were down 16% to 19%. Atlanta reported a slight increase in volume, while in the Kansas City Federal Reserve District, volume was about the same. In Chicago, volume was down slightly, and dollar sales were down 20% [216].

The New York Times business activity index closed the year at 63. It had been between 105 and 110 for the first nine months of 1929. Automobiles offered some hope of revival in 1932 due to low inventories [217].

Chapter 12

1932-1933: Final Collapse

The economy tumbled to incredible depths by the middle of 1932. Unemployment reached a staggering 25%. Agricultural prices, stock prices, and production statistics all fell through the first half of the year, finally hitting bottom in June and July. However, a modest revival occurred in the summer as domestic agricultural production had finally been cut by the steep price drops and abandonment of price supports in 1931. The stock market doubled in value over a two month period.

Unfortunately, the promise of a bona fide recovery evaporated in the second half of the year as agricultural prices dropped to new lows. Large tax increases undoubtedly added a heavy weight to the economy just when economic indicators had finally started to turn around. The election of Franklin Delano Roosevelt in November added to an environment of great uncertainty and unrest [254, p. 235-237]. Rumors of FDR's intent to abandon the U.S. gold standard, which he did nothing to deny, led to a complete collapse of the banking system in the first two months of 1933 [254, p. 324], [21, pp. 324-328].

12.1 More Credit and Monetary Inflation

With confidence in the dollar seemingly restored, Hoover sought to pump more credit into the economy in an effort to jump-start it. The first major program in this goal was the establishment of the Reconstruction Finance Corporation (RFC) in January 1932. A replacement of the NCC, the RFC was authorized to make loans to banks and railroads that were in need of credit to stay afloat. The RFC received an appropriation of $500,000,000 and was authorized to loan up to $2,000,000,000 [254, p. 296]. Although bank runs initially dropped considerably after its formation, the RFC was not particularly successful; it served principally to prevent the liquidation of businesses that probably needed to be liquidated[1] [254, p. 296], [41, pp. 58-59]. It was plagued by political favoritism, and later requirements to disclose loan recipients eventually resulted in runs on the companies that took RFC loans [21, p. 325].

A return to cheap money also occurred in 1932. The New York Fed lowered its discount rate to 3% on February 26 and $2\frac{1}{2}$% on June 25 [232]. The money supply did not expand as intended, however, because many banks, having seen the carnage of bank runs in 1930 and 1931, opted to maintain reserves well in excess of their legal requirements [254, pp. 302-304], [21, p. 323].

Under Congressional pressure, the Federal Reserve commenced a large-scale program of monetizing government debt. From April 6 to August 17, $1,000,000,000 of government debt was purchased by the Federal Reserve and used to back an equivalent issue of Federal Reserve notes [232], [5, pp. 257-258], [21, pp. 322-324, 384-389]. With the French press expressing doubts about the ability of the United States to maintain the gold standard, the inflation program backfired almost immediately; a rapid gold drain commenced in April and continued until the middle of June as France withdrew nearly all of its credits in the U.S. [224] The nation's gold stock fell 10.3% to $3.9 billion, pushing the money supply/gold ratio to 11.5, nearly matching its October 1931 peak. The economy was dragged further down with the renewed foreign doubts about the soundness of the dollar.

12.2   Revenue Act of 1932

With a $2.7 billion federal budget deficit developing, the Hoover administration determined at the start of 1932 that the budget needed to be rebalanced [254, pp. 286-288]. Unfortunately, significant spending reduc-

---

[1]In fairness, government trade barriers bore significant responsibility for the financial difficulties of the companies that took RFC loans; thus, it might seem appropriate that the same government should provide assistance to alleviate those difficulties (constitutional questions aside). However, such a policy could only work if the trade barriers were removed in short order (a difficult task even if the government actually wanted to achieve it); otherwise, the RFC would only postpone the inevitable, making things worse in the long run.

tion does not seem to have been seriously considered; instead, a wide array of tax hikes were enacted in the Revenue Act of 1932, which was passed by Congress and signed by Hoover on June 6. The tax hikes were projected to raise $1.1 billion in revenue. The act retroactively raised the top marginal income tax rate for 1932 from 25% to a whopping 63% [31]. Estate and gift taxes were raised. Excise taxes were levied on a wide assortment of articles, ranging from lubricating oils and brewers' wort to candy and electric energy for a two year period. Other articles, including telephone calls and bank checks, were also taxed for a two year period. Postal rates were raised for two years as well [222, 223]. Reversing the Mellon tax cuts of the 1920s, the 1932 tax hikes actually produced very little increase in government revenue (less than $73 million), as the economy suffered a new blow.

12.3   Final Stock Collapse

After holding fairly steady for the first three months of 1932, the stock market plunged yet again in April and May as the foreign gold drain restarted, foreign tariffs were increased [5, p. 162], and the tax hikes were developed. The monthly percentage decline of 23.4% in the Dow for April 1932 is the third[2] largest on record (after September 1931). (The 20.3% decline for May 1932 ranks seventh.) The market reached its bear market low on July 8, when the Dow closed at 41.22 (Tables 12.1 and 12.2). The Dow Jones average had fallen 89.2% from its September 1929 peak (Figure 12.1).

12.4   Summer Revival

The economy appeared to finally turn around in July. The stock market rallied sharply, with the Dow nearly doubling to 79.93 on September 7 (although still down 79% from the 1929 peak). Reports of smaller agricultural surpluses boosted agricultural prices, fueling the rally [5, p. 164-165]. The gold outflow abruptly reversed and became a steady gold inflow. Other indicators of business activity also turned around [233], leading many to believe (hope) that the bottom had *finally* been reached.

---

[2]March 1938 ranks second at 23.7%. The 23.6% decline of December 1914 is not counted here because that decline reflected resumption of trading after a $4^1/_2$ month suspension.

FRIDAY, JULY 8, 1932				
Company	Stock Price	%YTD	Annual Dividend Rate	Dividend Yield
Agricultural Equipment				
Case (J.I.) & Co.	$22^5/_8$	−44.6%	0		0.0%
International Harvester	$10^1/_2$	−56.2%	1.80		17.1%
Autos				
Auburn Auto	$44^7/_8$	−65.7%	4	+8% stk	8.9%
General Motors	$7^3/_4$	−65.7%	1		12.9%
Foods				
Coca-Cola	77	−28.0%	8†		10.4%
General Foods	$20^1/_8$	−40.8%	2		9.9%
National Biscuit	$21^3/_8$	−46.7%	2.80		13.1%
Mining				
Anaconda Copper	4	−59.5%	0		0.0%
Kennecott Copper	$6^1/_8$	−45.6%	0		0.0%
Railroads				
New York Central	11	−62.1%	0		0.0%
Pennsylvania R.R.	7	−61.4%	0		0.0%
Southern Pacific	$7^1/_4$	−73.9%	0		0.0%
Southern Railway	$3^1/_2$	−53.3%	0		0.0%
Union Pacific	$28^1/_2$	−59.9%	6		21.1%
Retail				
Safeway Stores	$30^3/_4$	−29.1%	5		16.3%
Sears Roebuck	$10^1/_4$	−68.9%	0		0.0%
Woolworth	$23^1/_8$	−42.2%	2.40		10.4%
Steel				
Bethlehem Steel	$8^3/_8$	−55.3%	0		0.0%
U.S. Steel	$21^1/_2$	−44.3%	0		0.0%
Utilities				
Public Service, N. J.	$28^7/_8$	−46.8%	3.20		11.1%
Southern Cal. Edison	$18^5/_8$	−40.9%	2		10.7%
Other Industries				
American Tobacco, B	$50^1/_8$	−28.1%	6†		12.0%
General Electric	$9^3/_8$	−62.5%	0.40		4.3%
Radio Corporation	$3^5/_8$	−34.1%	0		0.0%
Standard Oil of N. J.	24	−13.9%	2†		8.3%
United Aircraft & Tr	$7^5/_8$	−32.2%	0		0.0%
† – includes extra dividend				

Table 12.1: Selected stock prices at market close, July 8, 1932 [225]

Figure 12.1: Dow Jones Industrial Average, 1929 - 1932 [16]

FRIDAY, JULY 8, 1932			
Company/Issue	Bond Price	Current Yield	Yield to Maturity
Railroads			
New York Central 5s2013	$36^3/_4$	13.6%	13.6%
Pennsylvania R.R. $4^1/_2$s1970	42	10.7%	11.0%
Southern Pacific $4^1/_2$s1968	$32^1/_8$	14.0%	14.2%
Southern Railway 4s1956	$13^1/_4$	30.2%	30.4%
Union Pacific 4s1968	68	5.9%	6.2%
Utilities			
Public Service E&G $4^1/_2$s1970	97	4.6%	4.7%
Other Industries			
Bethlehem Steel 5s1936	80	6.2%	11.4%
General Motors 6s1937	$101^1/_2$	5.9%	5.7%
Standard Oil of N.J. 5s1946	$101^3/_4$	4.9%	4.8%

Table 12.2: Selected bond prices at market close, July 8, 1932 [226]

12.5   Autumn Disappointment

Unfortunately, the recovery was not maintained. Although an equilibrium appeared to have been reached at last, the situation was still very shaky. The public posting of RFC recipients in August revealed unexpected weaknesses in many companies, sapping confidence. The posting of the loan recipients also rendered the RFC ineffective, as recipients were "branded as unsound" and potential borrowers avoided taking out RFC loans to forestall the same fate [21, p. 325]. Increased tariffs around the world and protected agricultural markets abroad resulted in a huge global wheat surplus that undercut the summer price rallies when the surplus was reported in October [5, p. 172]. Calls for dollar devaluation from many in Congress discouraged investment[3] [249]. Business activity would remain fairly constant into December [233], but the stock market started to sag again. The upcoming presidential campaign portended great uncertainties about future government intervention.

12.6   War Debt Defaults

Senator William E. Borah (R-Idaho) had been particularly outspoken for many months in identifying the war debts and trade barriers as prime causes of the depression [5, p. 138, 163], but he was unable to change many opinions in Congress. With Congress clearly unwilling to renegotiate the war debts, neither Hoover nor FDR had authority to extend the Moratorium [232]. Hoover informed the debtor nations that they were expected to make their December 15 installment payments, even as the Depression made the burden ever heavier (Table 12.3). Great Britain ($95,550,000), Czechoslovakia, Finland, Italy, Lithuania, and Latvia made the payments, while France, Belgium, Estonia, Hungary, and Poland did not. The vote of the French Chamber to default on the debt payment also ousted French Premier Herriot from office [230], [231].

---

[3]The threats of dollar devaluation had a similar impact on the economy in the 1873-78 and 1893-96 depressions. The resumption of specie payments in 1879 and the defeat of "Free Silver" candidate William Jennings Bryan in the 1896 election definitively ended such threats in most minds and inaugurated robust economic recoveries [250].

Nation	Remaining Principal (million $)	1932 National Product(million $)	Debt/Product Ratio
Belgium	401	12,800 (NNP)	3%
Britain	4,398	12,500 (GDP)	35%
France	3,864	10,430 (GDP)	37%
Italy	2,005	5,630 (GNP)	36%
Others	267	-	-
Total	5,400	-	-

Table 12.3: War debts owed to United States after World War I

12.7   Banking Collapse of 1933

After Franklin Delano Roosevelt won the 1932 presidential election, rumors began swirling that he would devalue the dollar. As FDR did nothing to dispel the rumors, runs on banks and gold began anew by January 1933 and accelerated rapidly in February [21, pp. 324-328]. Unlike the bank runs of 1930 and 1931, a significant portion of the withdrawals was in gold coin. The declaration of state banking holidays in Nevada on October 31, 1932 and Iowa on January 20, 1933 only further hastened runs in the other states [254, p. 325-328], [21, p. 325]. By the time FDR was inaugurated on March 4, most banks in 35 states[4] had closed, with some bank closures in 4 other states and restrictions on withdrawals (generally 5% of deposits) prevalent elsewhere [235, 236].

With the banking and monetary system collapsing, the economy tumbled to new lows.

---

[4]Statewide bank closures took place in 21 states, including New York, on March 4 alone [236].

Chapter 13

1933-1941: Continuing Depression

President Franklin Delano Roosevelt was likely the most radical President in U.S. history. Within 100 days after taking office, he and the 73rd Congress had destroyed the currency, disregarded private property rights by abrogating private contracts, and established central economic planning agencies to dictate prices and wages [41, pp. 99-144]. The fact that the economy failed to substantially improve for the rest of the decade should not be surprising; a slow improvement from 1933 to 1937 ended with a sharp fall as Federal Reserve monetary tightening measures to curb increasing inflation culminated in the "Roosevelt Recession" of 1938 and unemployment again rising toward 20%.

With the outbreak of World War II in Europe, domestic economic problems became secondary to the need to stop the expanding tyranny of Adolf Hitler. The country focused on the need to provide troops for the war and supplies for the troops. FDR did, in fact, replace many of his "Brain Trust" advisers from the 1930s with experienced businessmen in order to boost wartime production [41, pp. 163-164]. After the war, world leaders recognized the importance of breaking down trade barriers between nations; as a result, economies prospered, and the return of chronic depression, which was feared by many, did not take place [6].

13.1   Gold Standard Abandonment and Gold Criminalization

On March 6, President Roosevelt declared a three-day national banking holiday and suspended redemption of dollars for gold and gold exports [21, p. 328]. FDR cited the Trading with the Enemy Act of 1917 to justify his actions [254, p. 328]. The Emergency Banking Act of March 9 retroactively authorized Roosevelt's actions; the act also criminalized the "hoarding" of gold and currency with a $10,000 fine and 10 years imprisonment [237], [238]. The suspension of gold convertibility and the provision of $200 million in additional Federal Reserve notes by the Emergency Banking Act enabled about 69% of the roughly 17,300 commercial banks in the U.S. to reopen under federal licensing March 13, 14, and 15. 11% reopened by June 30, and another 8% would eventually reopen by the end of 1936. The remainder never reopened – their assets were liquidated or merged into other banks [21, pp. 422-426].

On April 5, FDR, by executive order, invoked the Emergency Banking Act of March 9 to explicitly criminalize the possession of gold and gold certificates in excess of $100 by American citizens after May 1, except for rare coins and "reasonable amounts" for industrial or artistic uses [21, p. 463], [239]. The Secretary of the Treasury later issued an order on December 28 that further criminalized all possession of gold, except for rare coins, after January 17, 1934 [241]. $20.67 was provided for each ounce of gold that was turned in. The justification for these actions was questionable to say the least – and an assault on the Constitution[1] [24, pp. 108-123]. (I am hard pressed to think of a more tyrannical act by a U.S. President than this robbery[2] of the American people's money.)

The foreign exchange rate of the dollar remained near gold parity for over a month as most viewed the suspension of gold convertibility as temporary, and U.S. gold reserves were still substantial [5, p. 279], [21, pp. 462-463]. However, on April 19, FDR announced his intent to deliberately devalue the dollar, crashing the dollar's value in exchange markets [21, pp. 464-465], [240]. There was a temporary flurry of economic activity as businesses and consumers rushed to make purchases before the dollar fell fur-

---

[1] Article I, Section 10: "No State shall ... make any Thing but gold and silver Coin a Tender in Payment of Debts"

[2] robbery (n.) - "larceny from the person or presence of another by violence or threat" [38]

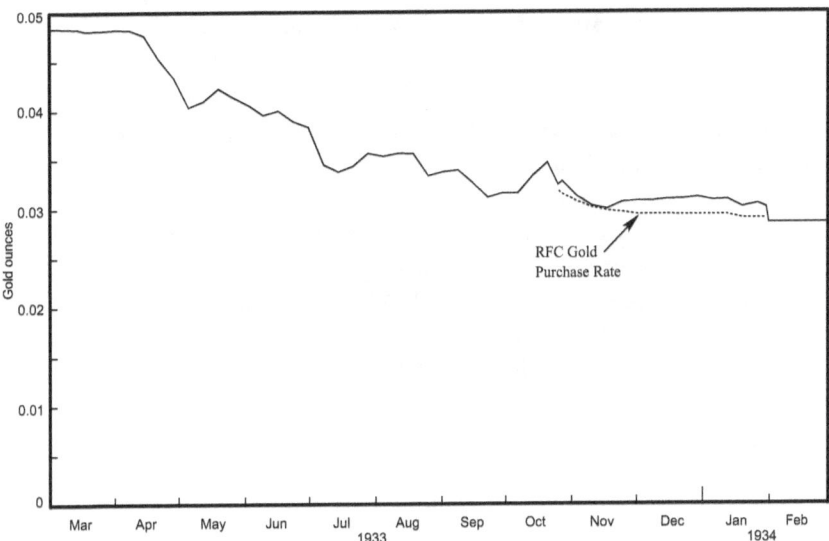

Figure 13.1: Weekly value of U.S. dollar in gold ounces, as indicated by franc exchange rate, 1933 - 1934 [248]

ther, but the economy went back into contraction by the fall [5, pp. 280-283, 296-297]. The dollar's value was allowed to "float" for nearly a year between $1/27$ oz. and $1/35$ oz. (Figure 13.1) Substantial gold purchases by the U.S. government starting in October significantly influenced the dollar's value [21, p. 465]. The passage of the Gold Reserve Act on January 30, 1934 authorized the President to fix the gold equivalent of the dollar at 50% to 60% of its pre-1933 value (i.e. between $1/41.34$ oz. and $1/34.45$ oz.). Roosevelt set the value of the dollar at $1/35$ ounce of gold (15.238 grains of gold 0.900 fine) the next day; however, only foreigners could convert gold into dollars at this rate. The dollar was thus repegged to gold but was no longer truly on a gold standard, since domestic holders of dollars could not redeem them for gold [21, pp. 469-474].

The dollar devaluation of 1933-34 meant that U.S. prices as "seen" by foreigners were cut by 40%. Not surprisingly, this change started an inrush of gold that would continue, with only one pause, for seven years. The gold inflow, however, did not result in a commensurate increase in the supply of dollars. U.S. gold holdings rose from $7.4 billion in February 1934 to $12.7 billion in 1937 – a 71% increase (Figure 13.3), but the increase in dollars over the same period was only 33% (Figure 13.2). Thus, the money supply/gold ratio, which was abruptly cut by the 1933-34 devaluation, continued to fall until 1937 (Figure 13.4). Certainly some new credit was created during this time, but not in proportion to the gold inflow. Although 1933-37 is considered a period of robust expansion by many, with GNP growing at 13% annually in current dollars [29] and a steady rise in stock prices (Figure 13.5), the steady drop in the money supply/gold and deposit-reserve ratios over this period are not signs of favorable business conditions. Unemployment recovered only slowly as FDR's programs set artificially high wages [41, pp. 99-110]. This period was a time of recovery from the banking collapse, but little real growth [5, pp. 297-301] (the GNP increase of 63% was less than the 67% increase that would be expected from the dollar devaluation.) No other period of expansion between 1867 and 1960 shows a comparable long-term decline in the deposit-reserve ratio [21, Chart 64].[3] The deposit-reserve ratio decline from 1933 to 1937 was in fact simply a continuation of the deflationary trend since 1929, as poor business conditions led to a lack of issuance of loans [21, pp. 495-496], [41, pp. 110-118]. Prices in terms of hard money (i.e. gold) were actually lower in 1936 than in 1932. Banks continued to maintain excess reserves throughout this period [5, pp. 301-309].

The devaluation of the dollar in 1933 was completely unnecessary for recovery and in all likelihood significantly hampered it. There is good reason to believe that the 1933 banking collapse would not even have occurred if FDR hadn't been intent on devaluation. Even after the banking collapse and emission of $200 million of additional paper money, foreign traders did not see any fundamental reason to believe that the dollar was overvalued, as prices had dropped steeply. Gold had been steadily flowing back into the United States throughout the second half of 1932, indicating that the dollar was, if anything, undervalued. Whereas monetary inflation creates short-term (false) prosperity at the cost of long-term growth [8], monetary deflation – as occurred from 1929-33 – generates short-term pain but retains excellent long-term prospects for growth. Having borne the pain of deflation in 1931 and 1932, the U.S. economy was at least in a position for rapid recovery[4] built on a stable currency, with lots of money waiting

---

[3]1891-92 shows a slight drop; sharp drops in the ratio occurred in 1948 and the end of 1950 during times of an otherwise gradual increase.

[4]The economy likely would not have returned to the prosperity of the 1920s without a reduction in international trade barriers, but at least the massive unemployment problem could have been addressed.

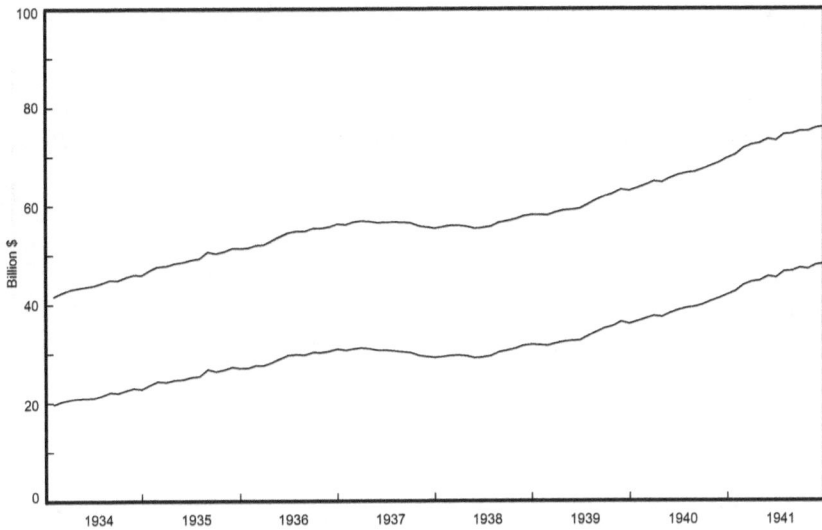

Figure 13.2: United States money supply, 1934 - 1941 [21]

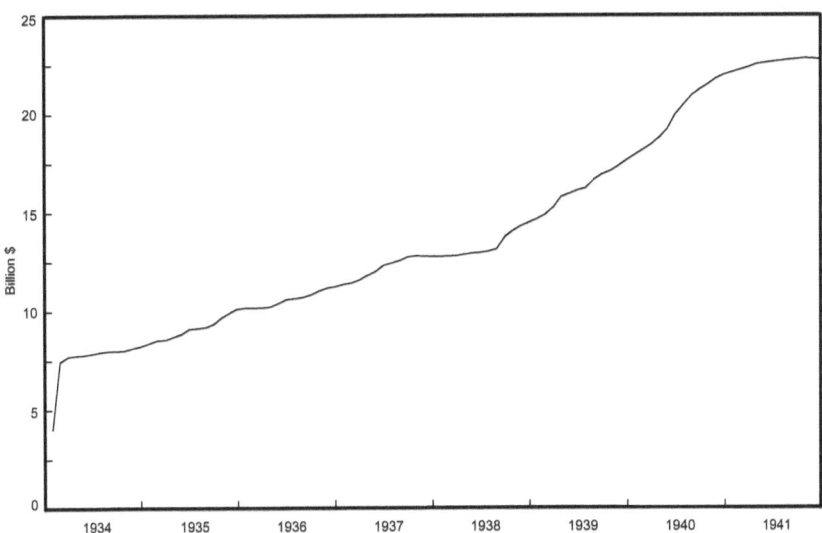

Figure 13.3: United States monetary gold stock, 1934 - 1941, including gold coin in circulation [12]

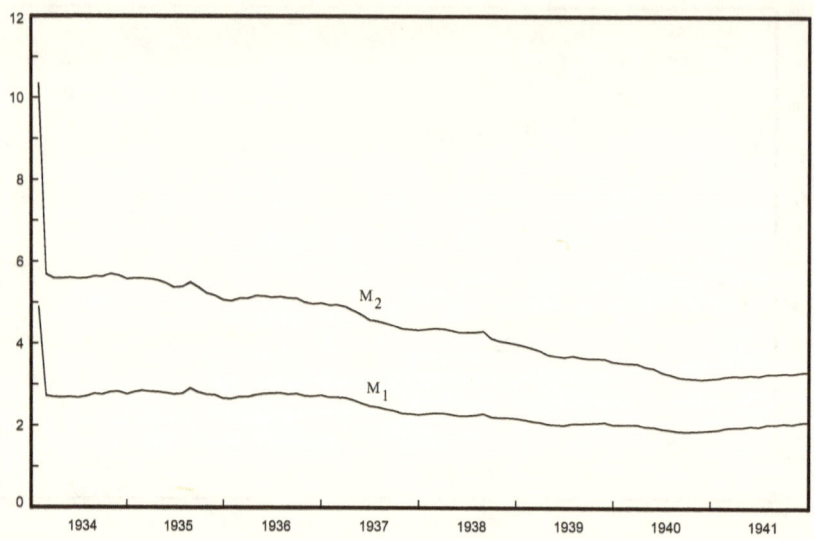

Figure 13.4: Ratio of money supply to monetary gold stock, 1934 - 1941

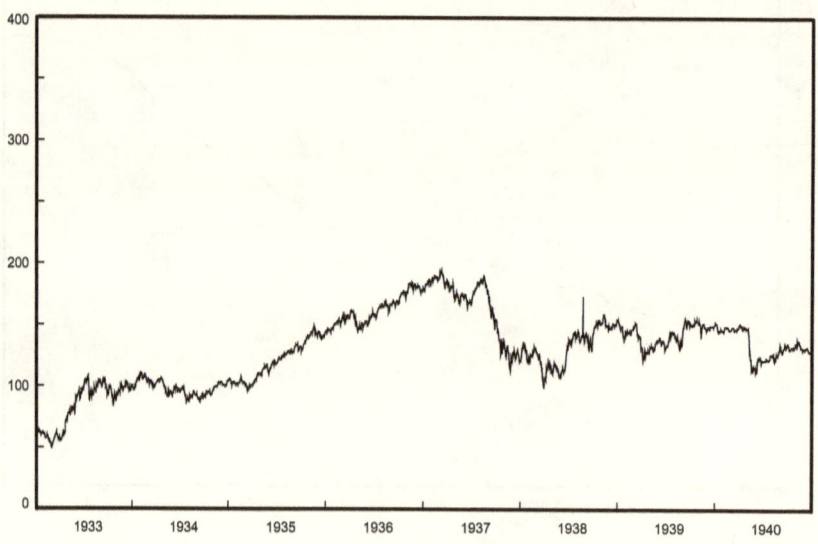

Figure 13.5: Dow Jones Industrial Average, 1933 - 1940 [16]

for good investment opportunities. The devaluation in 1933 instead gave the U.S. the worst of both worlds – the pain of the deflation from 1929 to 1933 and the lack of significant growth afterward. FDR's abrogation of the gold standard destroyed the opportunity for a normal recovery – and people's trust in the government as well. 141 years of a sound currency in the United States had ended, and the U.S. continues to pay the price for that to this day.

U.S. monetary policy from 1933 to 1936 was much like French monetary policy from 1926 to 1933. By maintaining an undervalued currency, gold was absorbed from the rest of the world in large quantities. French policy had perhaps exacerbated the problems of Great Britain in 1931, and U.S. policy subsequently helped force France off the gold standard in 1936 [5, pp. 279, 283-284, 314-315]. These policies of "competitive devaluations" further strangled world trade [253, pp. 116-119]. The clouds of war forming in Europe certainly didn't boost confidence either [253, pp. 196-198].

13.2   Deposit Insurance (FDIC)

The enactment of deposit insurance by Congress in 1933 meant that the federal government would back up to $2,500 of each bank deposit account starting January 1, 1934. The limit was quickly increased to $5,000 on July 1, 1934. The insurance would be provided by the Federal Deposit Insurance Corporation (FDIC), to which banks would contribute premiums equal to a set fraction of the insured deposits[5] [21, pp. 434-442]. Deposit insurance essentially ended the widespread bank runs which were common prior to 1933. However, it also allowed bankers to offload all of their risk onto the entire monetary and banking system while keeping the profits.

Deposit insurance also doesn't really prevent a wholesale banking collapse, since the government will allow the currency to be devalued as needed to pay depositors claims. (If a significant portion of the debts backing the currency go bad, a run on gold backing a gold standard currency will be unavoidable. The run can only be stopped by halting conversion or reducing the gold equivalent of the currency. Similarly, for a fiat currency, the extra money will simply be printed.) Depositors can thus get their money back during a widespread panic, but it may be of little real value. Deposit insurance strengthens the weaknesses of individual banks but sets

---

[5]Premiums were initially $1/2$ of 1% of insured deposits annually; the premium was subsequently set at $1/12$ of 1%.

up the entire banking and monetary system for a potential widespread collapse. The motivation behind deposit insurance is clearly understandable; however, deposit insurance overlooks the inherent instability of fractional reserve banking [255, p. 158].

13.3   "Depression Within the Depression" of 1937-38

The monetary inflation and the huge amounts of public spending from 1933 to 1937, combined with rumors of further dollar devaluation [21, p. 509], set the stage for a severe relapse of the Depression in 1937 and 1938, as stock prices fell 48% in seven months and unemployment jumped back up from 14% to 19%. With price inflation reaching 4.3% in the GNP deflator[6], bank reserve requirements were increased to prevent inflation from rapidly accelerating further [5, p. 304]. The cessation of gold inflow in latter 1937 and early 1938 despite a monetary contraction also indicates a lessening of confidence in the dollar. FDR's proposal to "pack the court" in early 1937 [41, pp. 117] could also have contributed to a general drop in confidence.

Once again, consumption – this time fueled by large public spending – had to be cut to match production, which was not keeping pace. Clearly, the public spending created at best meager additions to the value of the nation's productive capacity. The DJIA closing value of 98.95 on March 31, 1938 was, in terms of gold, less than its close of 58.80 on April 6, 1933.

The economic situation led Treasury Secretary Henry Morgenthau, Jr. to lament in May 1939 [41, p. 113]:

> "We have tried spending money. We are spending more than we have ever spent before and it does not work. And I have just one interest, and if I am wrong ... somebody else can have my job. I want to see this country prosperous. I want to see people get a job. I want to see people get enough to eat. We have never made good on our promises. ... I say after eight years of this Administration we have just as much unemployment as when we started. ... And an enormous debt to boot!"

---

[6]The inflation rate was 8.3% for the first half of the year [5, p. 304].

13.4   Prelude to World War II

The deposit-reserve ratio continued to drop from 1938 to 1940, when it finally reversed its long-term downward trend. By this time, the development of wartime trade with Britain began to impact the American economy [5, pp. 283, 320-321].

Chapter 14

Conclusions

1931 was a year of worldwide currency panic. As money is essential to a well-functioning economy [255, pp. 23-30], there should be no surprise that a depression of historic severity ensued. Yet much of the discussion about the start of the Great Depression to this day focuses on 1929 and the bursting of the stock market bubble. It is true that 1929 marked the start of 14 consecutive quarters of economic contraction [21, p. 197], [9]. However, the economy (and the stock market) did not free fall into an abyss. Both unemployment and price deflation were less severe in 1930 than in 1921. The markets rallied several times in 1930 and 1931 in anticipation of recovery, but each rally was followed by further decline when a true recovery failed to materialize [6]. It was only after the currency collapses in the fall of 1931 that the depression achieved historic status.

The trade walls erected prior to 1929 were sufficient to force a sharp economic adjustment[1]. However, it is questionable whether the depression would have become "Great" without the long list of economic blunders that followed the crash of 1929: Federal Farm Board price supports (1929-31); the Smoot-Hawley Tariff (1930); government coercion to avoid wage cuts (1929-32); significant increases in public spending (1930-32); and a

---

[1]Many commentators, ranging from Lou Dobbs [17] to even Murray Rothbard [254, p. 258], argue that the impact of the international trade barriers only played a small part in the Great Depression since exports constituted just 6% of GDP. This argument ignores the fact that the U.S. exported goods which cost *less* than 6% of GDP to produce in exchange for goods that would have cost the U.S. *more* than 6% of GDP to produce domestically. Quantifying how much more is beyond the scope of this book, but it could easily have been 2 or 3 (or more) times the price of the imports.

mammoth tax hike (1932). With so many bad policies implemented simultaneously, it is difficult to evaluate the individual impact of each policy.
With a cheap money policy in place throughout 1930 and 1931, the cu-
mulative impact of these policies was borne by the currencies; when the
currencies finally broke in 1931, the depression was amplified. By allowing
the destruction of the currency, economic damage well in excess of what
was caused by the 1920s tariff policy mistakes resulted.

The currency panics that occurred in 1931 were fundamentally a result
of a long-term economic reduction that revealed the inherent instability
of the fractional reserve banking system [255, p. 104]. The situation was
amplified by attempts to nominally define the currency in terms of gold
weights while circulating currency in amounts well in excess of the actual
gold to back it up. (At least in a fiat system, the value of the currency can
adjust continuously to reflect the creditworthiness of the issuing country.
These adjustments, however, can themselves discourage trade and economic
growth [5, p. 285].)

The major causes of the long-term economic reduction of the 1930s were
the growing international trade barriers and the rise of statist government
policies throughout the world. Deteriorating economic conditions spurred
a vicious cycle of proposals for more government barriers to commerce – inflation, higher taxes, higher tariffs – which in turn prompted economic conditions to deteriorate further. Hoover acknowledged the depressing effect
that "legislative uncertainty" had on the economy [79]. With the specter of
the Russian Revolution, Mussolini, and Hitler in the minds of many, fears
of reckless government increased throughout the 1930s [253, pp. 57-58] –
fears which in the end were proved to be justified. Continued political
uncertainty discouraged investment.

The fractional reserve banking system combined with a gold standard
currency attempted to equate the value of debt to an asset (gold). The long-
term contraction reduced the value of that debt, yet the nominal value
of the currency did not change. As prices fell throughout 1929-33 and
creditworthiness of borrowers dropped, gold wasn't gaining value nearly so
much as the debt backing paper money was losing it. Such a situation
exposes the inherent instability of the fractional reserve banking system.
The deflation of the money supply due to bank suspensions and currency
withdrawals alleviated somewhat the stress on the currency; however, it
also amplified the price drops, jeopardizing the value of more of the loans
backing the currency.

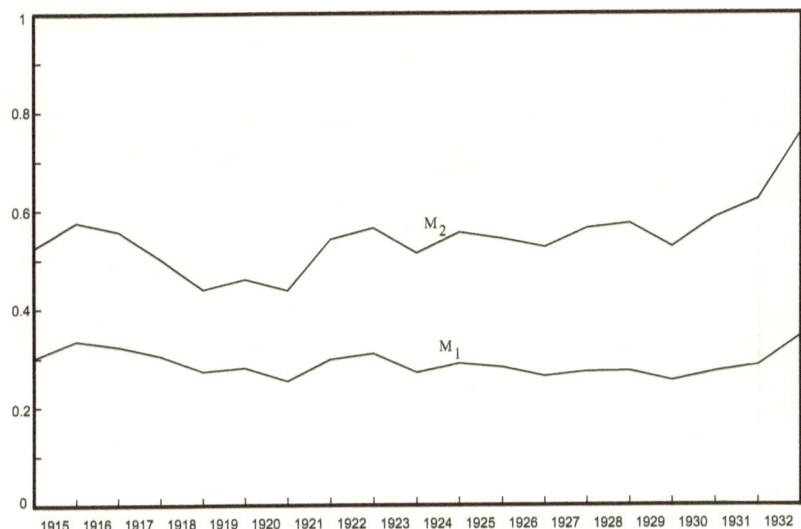

Figure 14.1: Ratio of money supply to gross national product, 1915 - 1932

The instability was particularly amplified by the heavy debt loads from World War I. As prices dropped, the impact of the high debts was magnified. With the deflation, the debts were contracts to pay a large proportion of the existing gold supply. In terms of gold, the debts, which had been contracted at a time of an inflated money supply, were now overvalued. Without fractional reserve banking, those debts would have been a much smaller proportion of the existing gold stock. (The "deflated" prices were actually closer to "reality.")

The ratio of the money supply to gross national product (Figure 14.1) offers an indication of the stress on the currency. This ratio has relevance because most of the currency is backed by debt, and the value of debt is dependent on future production. The M_2/GNP ratio alone, however, is not nearly sufficient to determine whether confidence in the currency will be sustained. This measurement does, however, show that monetary stress increased significantly from the 1920s and continued to grow steadily as the Depression deepened. A look at this ratio over the last 100 years shows that the Great Depression was the period of the greatest monetary stress in the United States (Figure 14.2).

The currency collapse of 1931 occurred despite significant price defla-

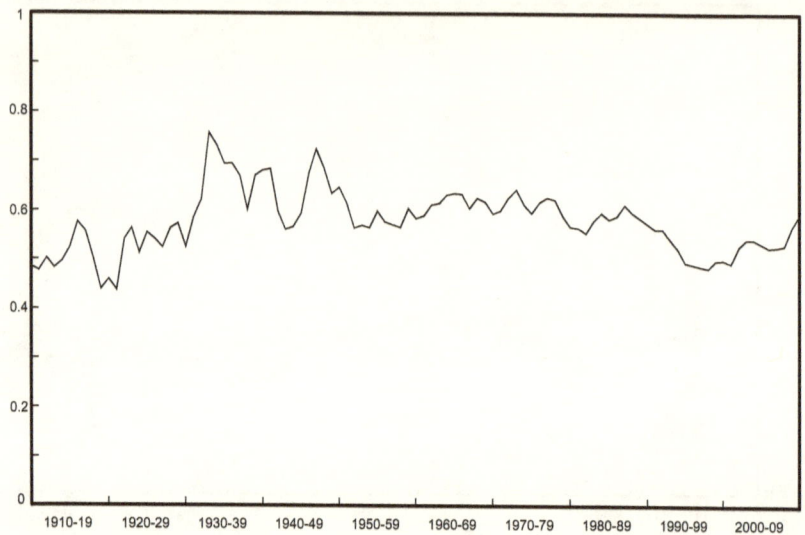

Figure 14.2: Ratio of money supply to gross national product, 1910 - 2009 [21, 29]

tion. In fact, prices were initially not allowed to fall far enough fast enough because of various government actions, such as agricultural price supports and a cheap money policy. These policies maintained uneconomic production, resulting in large surpluses that hung over the markets and produced a prolonged state of limbo. The continuing economic funk sapped confidence over time and led to further monetary and price deflation as banks folded and depositors withdrew their funds. As aptly noted by Robbins [253, p. 72], the threat of a price crash turned out to be worse than the price crash itself.

Robbins observed in 1934 that, under contemporary economic policy: "We eschew the sharp purge. We prefer the lingering disease." [253, p. 73] There is ample evidence to indicate that the "lingering disease" is far more detrimental to confidence and long-term economic performance than the "sharp purge" which is so feared today. The sharp declines of 1920-21 and 1987, for example, were followed by rapid recovery and strong growth, whereas the attempt to moderate the decline in 1930-31 ultimately decimated confidence and ended up putting the economy into the longest and deepest depression in American history.

Contrary to Freidman and Schwartz [21], it wasn't a declining money supply that caused catastrophic economic contraction; rather, it was a bad economy that deflated the money supply [41, pp. 72-74], [5, pp. 241-245]. With business conditions remaining poor for an extended time, more and more depositors withdrew money from the banks. Because of the fractional reserve banking system, these withdrawals forced a contraction of the money supply. The contraction of the money supply in 1920-21 was sharper than in 1929-30, yet the former was followed by a period of strong economic growth.

Economics is defined as "a social science concerned chiefly with description and analysis of the production, distribution, and consumption of goods and services" [38]. Money plays a vital role in matching production and consumption, but ultimately it is the production that creates wealth. Inflating the money supply to alleviate recessions and depressions is an attempt to preserve the existing consumption and production structure – which, as evidenced by a recession's occurrence, is unsustainable. Attempts to inflate out of a depression are thus doomed to fail.

Many people point to the Great Depression as a consequence of "unfettered" market forces. This criticism is clearly ignorant of the historical record (there were no depressions of comparable severity prior to Hoover's unprecedented government intervention in the economy) and also ignores the fact that markets are inherently stable and self-balancing, since all transactions occur voluntarily [255, pp. 23-24]. Governments can (and indeed must) facilitate commerce, but they must treat buyer and seller equally in order to do so.

Had true market forces been allowed to operate following the crash of '29, there is no doubt that the subsequent economic correction would have been sharper and initially deeper. However, it also would have had a chance to stabilize much sooner. In particular, the crop surpluses of 1930 and 1931 would not have been so incredibly huge. Instead, the government artificially boosted prices for crops and tried to inflate the currency even further, blatantly ignoring the economic reality that much of what was being grown was no longer of much value – thanks, in no small part, to the autarkic worldwide trade war. The growing stress between economic realities and government wishes meant that the value of the currency – the remaining "unconstrained variable in the economic equation" – would bear the brunt of the necessary adjustments.

In the U.S., confidence in the dollar was propped up by monetary austerity in October 1931. So why did recovery ultimately fail? After a steep drop necessitated by liquidation of unproductive enterprises, the U.S. economy appeared to hit bottom in July 1932 as agricultural surpluses were liquidated. However, the incredible tax hikes of 1932, debt monetization that undermined confidence in the dollar, and more foreign tariff hikes all combined to weigh down the economy in the second half of the year. The impending presidency of FDR and widespread fears of government abrogation of the gold standard destroyed the banking system in the beginning of 1933.

It is not capitalism that is unstable – the observed instability comes from a fractional reserve banking system that attempts to fix the value of credit to a physical asset. The situation in the early 1930s was exacerbated by the monetary inflation of the preceding decade. When depositors sought to lawfully redeem their currencies in gold, they discovered that their legal claims were little more than pieces of paper [254, pp. 324-327], [255, pp. 51-60]. With commensurate monetary deflation[2], the processes of bankruptcy and debt restructuring, allowing for liquidation of unproductive capital while allowing profitable business operations to continue, are a suitable resolution of such situations [249], although they are admittedly somewhat cumbersome and require time. The alternative resolution by the expedient of currency devaluation is a socialization of the bankruptcy of debtors – creating a "moral hazard" by encouraging future irresponsibility.

The Great Depression demonstrated the importance of currency to the economy. A long period of deepening economic decline, and government attempts to defy reality, steadily added stress to the world's currencies. In 1931, that stress reached the breaking point, unleashing economic havoc of historic proportions.

---

[2]Yes, this means that depositors would likely suffer some losses. However, since they have been earning a return on their money, shouldn't they bear some of the risk if that money was invested as they intended?

Chapter 15

2001- : Repeating History?

Since George W. Bush was inaugurated in 2001, Federal Reserve policy has been decidedly inflationary [10], [30, pp. 274-276]. The price of gold has risen from $265/oz. in 2001 to $1100/oz. at the end of 2009. Oil has risen from $29/barrel to $78/barrel over the same period [243]. Unlike the 1920s, however, there have been large increases in government spending for the post-9/11 wars, a new prescription drug entitlement program, and various domestic federal programs [2,258]. Taxes are also considerably higher than the 1920s (there were no FICA or Medicare taxes back then). Accordingly, by most perceptions, economic prosperity has not grown at nearly the pace of the 1920s; it is highly doubtful that the decade will be remembered as the "Roaring 00's."

The inflation culminated in a dramatic market crash in September and October of 2008 and a sharp decline in economic output. The political response to the recession has been eerily similar to the government policies of the early 1930s. The Troubled Asset Relief Program (TARP) looks very much like a reincarnation of the Reconstruction Finance Corporation (RFC) of 1932. Since the market crash of 2008, the Federal Reserve has maintained a cheap money policy with a record low discount rate – just as it did in 1930 and 1931[1]. The government has used home buyer tax

---

[1]In the 19th century, Walter Bagehot's dictum for monetary policy in a crisis was that the central bank should provide essential liquidity by discounting "freely but at a high rate of discount." [41, p. 74] This rule was obviously violated in both 1930-31 and

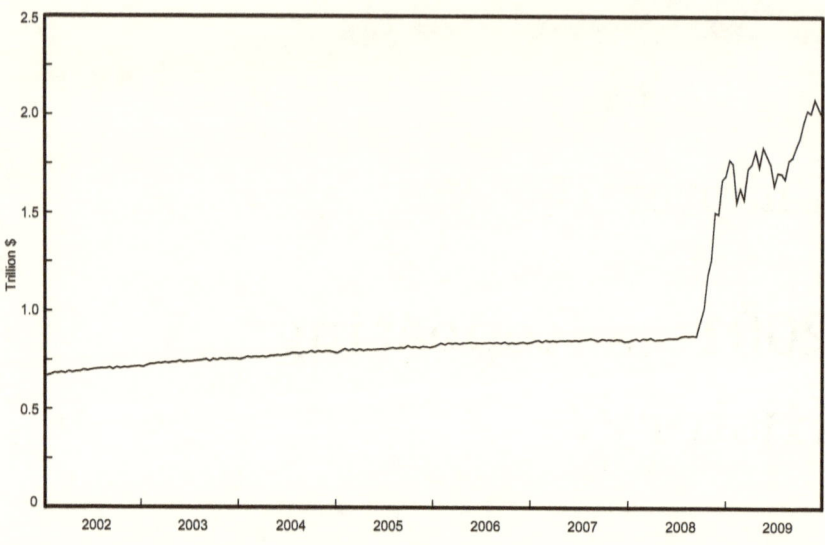

Figure 15.1: Federal Reserve monetary base, 2002 - 2009 [19]

credits and mortgage "modifications" (essentially legalized abrogations of contracts to lenders) to artificially prop up housing prices – much like the agricultural price supports of the Federal Farm Board in the early 1930s. Led by a $787 billion "stimulus" package, Federal government spending has been dramatically increased – much like 1930 and 1931. This spending is being financed by debt that is being monetized by the Federal Reserve at an alarming rate (Figure 15.1) – like the April 1932 open-market purchase program, but on a much larger scale. Large tax increases – similar to the Revenue Act of 1932 – may soon be implemented, and taxes will rise in 2011 if Congress simply does nothing. The threats of more Federal government statism, such as health care "reform" and carbon cap-and-trade hang over the economy like the Sword of Damocles – uncertainties about foreign trade and political stability in Europe (and more Federal government statism) had a similar effect in the early 1930s. The unemployment rate of 8.7% for 1930 is very similar to the average unemployment rate in 2009 (around 9%).

A debt crisis erupted in a small European nation with generous social benefits (Austria) about 19 months after the 1929 stock market crash.

2008.

Recently – about 19 months after the 2008 financial crisis – a debt crisis erupted in a small European nation with generous social benefits (Greece).

There are a few significant differences between now (2009-10) and then (1930-31). The worldwide mistrust between foreign nations that generated an autarkic drive toward self-sufficiency in the early 1930s is largely absent today. Political instability in central Europe is also not present today – virtually no one is worried that a Nazi regime will soon take power in Germany. These two factors indicate that an economic calamity as severe as the Great Depression is unlikely now. On the minus side, there are enormously expensive ($100,000,000,000,000,000) [3] Federal retirement entitlements and municipal pension benefits in place now that were not present then. These benefits include automatic cost-of-living adjustments based on price indices – a perfect engine of hyperinflation.

The monetary dynamics have also changed significantly since the start of the Great Depression. In 1930, the U.S. and most European nations still had a monetary gold standard; thus, paper currency was still valued as being nearly equal to gold up to the moment that gold redemptions were suspended. Also, as there was no deposit insurance in the U.S., the money supply shrank as banks were suspended and confidence in the remaining banks eroded. These two factors both acted to drive prices in dollars downward as the Depression deepened. Today, U.S. currency is a fiat money, with a daily floating of its value against gold and other currencies. Its value can thus gradually adjust over time to reflect inflation, unlike the early 1930s, when currency values remained fixed until the economic imbalances became large enough to produce dramatic gold crises and sudden, large currency devaluations [5, p. 285-286]. With deposit insurance having been in place since 1934, public confidence in the banks has largely been maintained, and hence a monetary contraction like that of 1930-31 has not occurred (Figure 15.2)[2]. As of September 2009, the FDIC insurance fund is bankrupt, meaning that all refunds of depositor money from failed banks are now financed by Treasury borrowing [18] (in effect printed money). Prices in dollars have risen significantly since bottoming out in March 2009 (although prices in terms of gold have not, indicating that many economically depressing factors are still present). The record low discount rates of 2008-09 have resulted in an expanded money supply and a concurrent

---

[2]In the current fiat money system with fractional reserve banking, bank deposits are partially backed by reserves consisting of base money, which is only emitted or absorbed by the Federal Reserve [32, pp. 49-50].

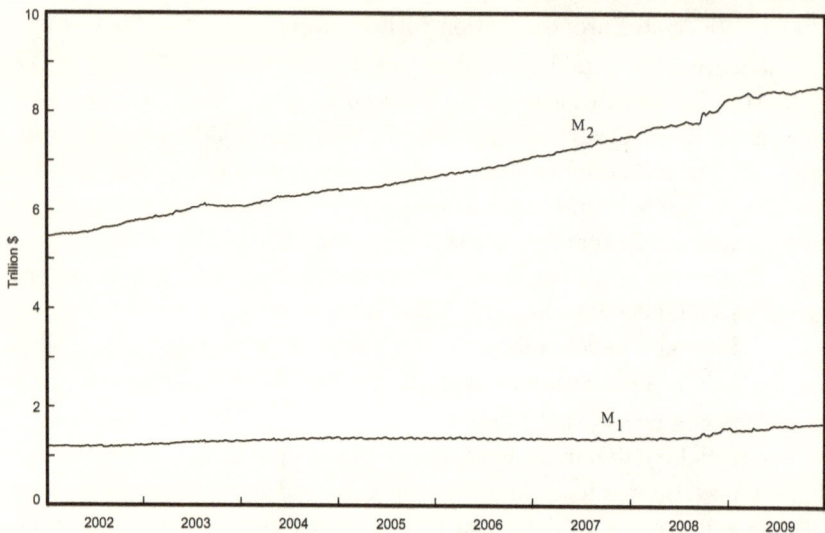

Figure 15.2: United States money supply, 2002 - 2009 [20]

modest rebound in economic activity. (The rebound has also been aided by a significant slowdown in the Congressional legislative agenda, reducing some of the political uncertainty that had significantly depressed the economy in late 2008 and early 2009.) It remains to be seen how much of this rebound is a reflection of new economically productive enterprises and how much is an inflation-driven continuation of past unproductive activities – or government creation of new unproductive activities[3]. (The fact that unemployment remains stubbornly high despite a ridiculously cheap money policy is not a good sign.)

Despite these differences, a currency collapse similar to 1931, characterized by an abrupt drop of 20% or more[4] in the dollar's value, appears likely in the not-too-distant future[5], unless there is an abrupt reversal of current

---

[3] How can an economy built on a foundation of unrealistically low interest rates be fundamentally sound?

[4] This estimate is based on the 1931 experience in sterling (the world's primary currency at the time) as well as the increase in the M_2/GDP ratio since the 1990s, when the dollar's value was stable.

[5] The exact timing is very difficult to predict with any accuracy; many observers believe that such a "day of reckoning" is still years away. However, several factors make September 2010 an interesting month to watch: 1. Depressed economic conditions will

U.S. monetary and fiscal policies. The huge increase in base money (greater than 150%) means that inflation is capable of accelerating $2\frac{1}{2}$ times faster, creating a potential "volcano of inflation" that will be difficult for the Federal Reserve to control. It is extremely doubtful that the Federal Reserve can withdraw all or even most of the base money that was created in the last year and a half – the Fed will almost certainly not be able to sell the government securities at a price nearly equal to the price at which they purchased them. Development of rapid inflation and higher interest rates could easily reduce the value of those securities by 50% or more. In such a scenario, interest rates would need to be rapidly hiked to very high levels to prevent a rapid and serious drop in the dollar's value.

Currently, many depressing factors, including political factors – uncertainty of government tax, health care, and carbon policies – are keeping a lid on inflation [37], and there is still a remarkable reservoir of confidence in the dollar's value, as evidenced by low interest rates on government securities and the hoarding of cash [4]. This reservoir is a result of 20 years of responsible management by the Federal Reserve in the 1980s and 1990s, when the dollar's value was stabilized and even increased. That stability was a foundation of the economic prosperity of those two decades. Even now, the U.S. dollar is still widely viewed as a yardstick of value. The dollar's value is currently sustained by faith – faith that its value will be maintained in the future. That faith can evaporate very quickly. (The stock market has repeatedly demonstrated how quickly faith in financial assets can erode.)

Currencies backed primarily by debt have been seen to be remarkably resilient throughout history; however, there is a limit to the amount of stress they can bear. The value of debt can depreciate significantly in depressed economic conditions. Although depression keeps prices down, prolonged depression can break confidence in debt-backed currency – as happened in 1931.

If a dollar crash is permitted to happen, the ensuing depression will be severe – far more severe than if monetary austerity had been maintained after the 2008 market crash. A stable currency, whether it be a commodity or a fiat currency, is an essential foundation of sound economic decisions

---

have persisted for almost two full years (just like September 1931); 2. financial crises have a history of occurring in the fall (1907, 1929, 1931, 1987, 2008); and 3. the 2011 tax increases will begin to considerably affect financial markets (like 1982 but in the opposite direction). (Prospects of change in Congress may offset – or enhance – these factors.)

and economic prosperity [5,30,255]. It will be difficult and costly to rebuild that foundation – the nation's credit and good name – if it is allowed to crumble away.

Appendix A

1913 Currency Unit Definitions and Parity Exchange Rates

Gold content of the currency was generally legally specified in grains (gr) in the United States. 1 troy ounce equals 480 grains, while 1 pound (avoirdupois) equals 7000 grains. For metric conversions, a grain is equal to 0.0648 grams.

Nation	Currency Unit	Definition	Units/ troy oz.	$/Unit [12]
United States	Dollar	25.8 grains of gold of .900 fineness (1900) [1, p. 144]	$20.67	$1
Canada	Dollar	One U.S. Dollar (1858) [265]	C$20.67	$1
Austria-Hungary	Crown	0.304878 g of gold[a] (1892)	102.02 Kr	$0.2026
Belgium	Franc	290.32 mg of gold[b] (1878)	107.14 fr	$0.1929
Denmark	Krona	$1/2480$ kg of gold[c] (1873)	77.14 Kr	$0.2680
France	Franc	290.32 mg of gold[b] (1878)	107.14 fr	$0.1929
Germany	Mark	1395 marks per pound (0.5 kg) of gold (1871) [1, p. 138]	M 86.78	$0.2382
Great Britain	Pound	113.00 grains of gold[d] (1816)	£4.2477	$4.8665
Italy	Lira	290.32 mg of gold[b] (1878)	L 107.14	$0.1929
Netherlands	Guilder	604.8 mg of gold[e] (1875)	ƒ 51.43	$0.4020
Norway	Krona	$1/2480$ kg of gold[c] (1875)	77.14 Kr	$0.2680
Russia	Ruble	774.235 mg of gold[f] (1897)	R 40.174	$0.5146
Spain	Peseta	290.32 mg of gold[b] (1878)	107.14 Pt	$0.1929
Sweden	Krona	$1/2480$ kg of gold[c] (1873)	77.14 Kr	$0.2680
Switzerland	Franc	290.32 mg of gold[b] (1878)	107.14 fr	$0.1929
Argentina	Peso	5 francs (1881) [263]	21.43 P	$0.9647
Japan	Yen	0.75 g of gold (1897) [267]	¥ 41.47	$0.4985

[a] The Austrian crown was defined as a gold equivalent of $1/3$ of a Vereinsthaler ($16\frac{2}{3}$ g of silver), with gold valued at a ratio of $18\frac{2}{9}$:1 to silver. The crown was therefore $1/3280$ kg of gold [264, 270].

[b] The franc was defined as 5 g of silver of .900 fineness by the French Monetary Law of 1803. Gold was valued at a $15\frac{1}{2}$:1 ratio to silver. The Latin Monetary Union was formed in 1865 by four nations (France, Belgium, Switzerland, and Italy) that agreed to use the same base unit of money. The countries transitioned from a bimetallic standard to a gold standard between 1873 and 1878 [1, p. 125,145,199].

[c] Scandinavian Monetary Union [269]

[d] £3 17s $10\frac{1}{2}$d per troy ounce of gold of $^{11}/_{12}$ (.9166+) fineness [32, p. 30], [253, p. 78]

[e] $9\frac{1}{3}$ grains [266]

^{f} $2^2/_3$ francs [268, 271]

Appendix B

1928 Currency Unit Definitions and Parity Exchange Rates

Nation	Currency Unit	Definition	Units/ troy oz.	$/Unit [12]
United States	Dollar	25.8 grains of gold of .900 fineness (1900) [1, p. 144]	$20.67	$1
Canada	Dollar	One U.S. Dollar (1858) [265]	C$20.67	$1
Austria-Hungary	Schilling	0.211721 g of gold[a] (1924)	S 146.91	$0.1407
Belgium	Franc	$1/175$ of £1[b] (1926)	743.40 fr	$0.0278
Denmark	Krona	$1/2480$ kg of gold (1873)	77.14 Kr	$0.2680
France	Franc	58.95 mg of gold (1928) [48]	527.63 fr	$0.0392
Germany	Mark	1395 marks per pound (0.5 kg) of gold (1871) [1, p. 138]	M 86.78	$0.2382
Great Britain	Pound	113.00 grains of gold (1816)	£4.2477	$4.8665
Italy	Lira	$1/19$ of $1 (1927) [46]	L 392.76	$0.0526
Netherlands	Guilder	604.8 mg of gold (1875)	ƒ 51.43	$0.4020
Norway	Krona	$1/2480$ kg of gold (1875)	77.14 Kr	$0.2680
Spain	Peseta	290.32 mg of gold (1878)	107.14 Pt	$0.1929
Sweden	Krona	$1/2480$ kg of gold (1873)	77.14 Kr	$0.2680
Switzerland	Franc	290.32 mg of gold (1878)	107.14 fr	$0.1929
Argentina	Peso	5 francs (1881) [263]	21.43 P	$0.9647
Japan	Yen	0.75 g of gold (1897) [267]	¥ 41.47	$0.4985

[a] The value of a paper crown was fixed at $1/14400$ of a gold (1892) crown in 1924 following hyperinflation in 1922 [42, 44]. The schilling was introduced at the end of 1924 with a value of 10,000 paper crowns [1, p. 16].

[b] The belga, a unit of gold currency for international transactions, was defined as 5 francs ($1/35$ of £1), or 0.209211 g of gold [45].

Bibliography

[1] Allen, Larry. *Encyclopedia of Money.* Santa Barbara, CA: ABC-CLIO, Inc., 1999.

[2] Bartlett, Bruce. *Impostor: How George W. Bush Bankrupted America and Betrayed the Reagan Legacy.* New York, NY: Doubleday, 2006.

[3] Bartlett, Bruce, "The 81% Tax Increase," *Forbes,* May 15, 2009. Available at `http://www.forbes.com/2009/05/14/taxes-social-security-opinions-columnists-medicare.html`. Retrieved July 23, 2010.

[4] Blake, Rich and Dalia Fahmy, "Hoarding, Not Hiring – Corporations Stockpile Mountain of Cash," *ABC News,* April 1, 2010. Available at `http://abcnews.go.com/Business/hoarding-hiring-corporations-stockpile-mountain-cash/story%3Fid%3D10250559`. Retrieved July 23, 2010.

[5] Blatt, Dan. *Understanding the Great Depression and the Modern Business Cycle.* Dan Blatt, 2009.

[6] Blatt, Dan, "Summaries of Controversies and Facts: The Great Deception," FUTURECASTS online magazine, Vol. 3, No. 4., April 1, 2001. Available at `http://www.futurecasts.com/Depression_mythology-I.html`.

[7] Blatt, Dan, "Book Review: *Irrational Exuberance* by Robert J. Schiller," FUTURECASTS online magazine, Vol. 3, No. 12., December 1, 2001. Available at `http://www.futurecasts.com/book%20review%2017.htm`.

[8] Blatt, Dan, "Understanding Inflation," FUTURECASTS online magazine, Vol. 6, No. 2., February 1, 2004.
Available at `http://www.futurecasts.com/Understanding%20 Inflation.html`.

[9] Blatt, Dan, "Book Review: *A Monetary History of the United States 1867-1960* by Milton Friedman and Anna Schwartz," FUTURECASTS online magazine, Vol. 9, No. 6., June 1, 2007.
Available at `http://www.futurecasts.com/Friedman,%20Monetary %20History%20of%20U.S.%20(II).htm`.

[10] Blatt, Dan, "Futurecasts for the 21st Century: Eleventh Annual Review of Futurecast Issues," FUTURECASTS online magazine, Vol. 12, No. 1., January 1, 2010.
Available at `http://www.futurecasts.com/Annual%20Futurecasts %20review.htm`.

[11] Blatt, Dan, "Monetary Inflation and Business Cycle Volatility," FUTURECASTS online magazine, Vol. 12, No. 2, February 1, 2010.
Available at `http://www.futurecasts.com/Business%20cycle%20 volatility.htm`.

[12] Board of Governors of the Federal Reserve System. *Banking and Monetary Statistics 1914-1941*. Washington, DC: Federal Reserve System, 1943.[1]
Available at `http://fraser.stlouisfed.org/publications/bms/`. Retrieved October 17, 2009.

[13] Board of Governors of the Federal Reserve System. *Federal Reserve Bulletin,* September 1937.
Available at `http://fraser.stlouisfed.org/publications/FRB/ issue/2413/`. Retrieved March 5, 2010.

[14] Callender, Harold. "The Eyes of Europe are Again on Germany," *New York Times,* May 31, 1931, p. XX1.

[15] Dixit, Avinash and Robert Pindyck. *Investment under Uncertainty.* Princeton, NJ: Princeton University Press, 1993.

---

[1]Per [21, pp. 463-464], $287 million of gold coin that was deducted in the derivation of the U.S. gold stock figures in this reference is added back into the U.S. gold stock figures throughout this book.

[16] Dow Jones, Dow Jones Industrial Average.
     Data from `http://www.analyzeindices.com/dowhistory/`
     `djia-100.txt`. Retrieved September 12, 2009.

[17] Economic Populist Forum, "Topic: Tariffs: The Smoot-Hawley Fairy
     Tale," February 29, 2008.
     Available at `http://unlawflcombatnt.proboards.com/index.cgi?`
     `board=globalization&action=display&thread=2528&page=1`.
     Retrieved August 3, 2010.

[18] Federal Deposit Insurance Corporation, Memorandum to Board of
     Directors from Arthur J. Murton, September 28, 2009.
     Available at `http://www.fdic.gov/news/board/Sept29no1.pdf`.
     Retrieved July 23, 2010.

[19] Federal Reserve Bank of St. Louis, Economic Research,
     "Series: BASE, St. Louis Adjusted Monetary Base,"
     `http://research.stlouisfed.org/fred2/series/BASE`. Retrieved
     April 3, 2010.

[20] Federal Reserve Bank of St. Louis, Economic
     Research, "Series: M2, M2 Money Stock,"
     `http://research.stlouisfed.org/fred2/series/M2`. Retrieved
     April 3, 2010.

[21] Friedman, Milton and Anna Schwartz. *A Monetary History of the
     United States, 1867-1960*. Princeton, NJ: Princeton University Press,
     1963.

[22] Galbraith, John Kenneth. *Money: Whence It Came, Where It Went*.
     London: Andre Deutsch, 1975.

[23] Gale Group, The. *Gale Encyclopedia of U.S. Economic History*.
     Farmington Hills, MI: The Gale Group, 1999.

[24] Gnazzo, Douglas V. *Honest Money: A History of United States Gold
     and Silver Currency*, e-book, 2008.
     Available at `http://www.honestmoneyreport.com/`. Retrieved April
     14, 2009.

[25] Goldberg, Jonah. *Liberal Fascism*. New York, NY: Broadway Books,
     2009.

[26] Greensburger, "GermanyHyperChart.jpg," July, 2009. Available at http://en.wikipedia.org/wiki/ File:GermanyHyperChart.jpg (public domain).

[27] James, Edwin L. "German Reparations and Allied War Debts," *New York Times,* June 14, 1931, p. XX1.

[28] Keynes, John M. *The Economic Consequences of the Peace.* London: McMillan, 1919. Reprint, New York, NY: Skyhorse Publishing, 2007.

[29] Kurian, George Thomas. *Datapedia of the United States 1790-2005,* 2nd ed. Lanham, MD: Bernan Press, 2001.

[30] Laffer, Arthur, Stephen Moore, and Peter Tanous. *The End of Prosperity.* New York: Threshold Editions, 2008.

[31] Laffer, Arthur B., "Taxes, Depression, and Our Current Troubles," *Wall Street Journal,* September 22, 2009, p. A25.

[32] Lewis, Nathan. *Gold: The Once and Future Money.* Hoboken, NJ: John Wiley & Sons, 2007.

[33] Little, Jeffrey and Lucien Rhodes. *Understanding Wall Street.* Cockeysville, MD: Liberty Publishing Company, 1978.

[34] Lokey, Eugene M., "Along the Highways of Finance," *New York Times,* August 2, 1931, p. N11.

[35] M. Ramsey King Securities, Inc., *The King Report,* Issue 3808, February 11, 2008. Available at http://anonymousmonetarist.blogspot.com/2008/ 11/history-of-first-great-depression.html. (Anonymous Monetarist, "History of the First Great Depression," November 29, 2008). Retrieved September 3, 2009.

[36] Machlup, Fritz, "The Consumption of Capital in Austria," *Review of Economic Statistics, 11,* 1935, pp. 13-19. Available at http://mises.org/resources/998. Retrieved July 19, 2010.

[37] Meltzer, Allan H., "Why Obamanomics Has Failed," *Wall Street Journal,* June 30, 2010, p. A21.

[38] Merriam-Webster Inc. *Webster's Ninth New Collegiate Dictionary.* Springfield, MA: Merriam-Webster, 1990.

[39] Mitchell, Brian. *International Historical Statistics: Europe 1750-1993.* New York: Stockton Press, 1998.

[40] Muravchik, Joshua. *Heaven on Earth.* San Francisco, CA: Encounter Books, 2002.

[41] Murphy, Robert. *The Politically Incorrect Guide to the Great Depression and the New Deal.* Washington, DC: Regnery Publishing, Inc., 2009.

[42] *New York Times,* "Gold Premium in Austria," April 8, 1923, p. S7.

[43] *New York Times,* "Dawes Committee Report in Full by Cable," April 10, 1924, pp. 9-13.

[44] *New York Times,* "New Ministry Watched by Financial Vienna," December 8, 1924, p. 30.

[45] *New York Times,* "Belgian money will go on a new gold basis ...," October 26, 1926, p. 5.

[46] *New York Times,* "Italy Fixes Lira on Gold Standard," December 22, 1927, pp. 1, 3.

[47] *New York Times,* "Members of President Coolidge's Cabinet Review Work and Accomplishments of Department During Last Twelve Months – Forecast Future," January 1, 1928, p. N4.

[48] *New York Times,* "To Stabilize Franc at 25.52 to Dollar," June 24, 1928, pp. 1, 25.

[49] *New York Times,* "Wheat Prices Drop Below the Dollar," May 28, 1929, p. 59.

[50] *New York Times,* "Full Debt Accord Reached; Belgium Agrees to Settle Marks Issue with Germany," June 5, 1929, pp. 1-2.

[51] *New York Times,* "Wheat Value Rises $68,000,000 in Day," July 16, 1929, p. 36.

[52] *New York Times,* "Wheat Prices Drop After Early Rise," July 30, 1929, p. 40.

[53] *New York Times,* "Wheat Prices Rise in Active Market," August 2, 1929, p. 37.

[54] *New York Times,* "Farm Machinery Boosts Production," August 18, 1929, p. 16.

[55] *New York Times,* "Transactions on the New York Stock Exchange, Tuesday, September 3, 1929," September 4, 1929, pp. 40, 43.

[56] *New York Times,* "Bond Sales on the Stock Exchange, Tuesday, September 3, 1929," September 4, 1929, p. 45.

[57] *New York Times,* "Losses Recovered in Part," October 25, 1929, pp. 1-2.

[58] *New York Times,* "Premier Issues Hard Hit," October 29, 1929, pp. 1-2.

[59] *New York Times,* "Transactions on the New York Stock Exchange, Monday, October 28, 1929," October 29, 1929, pp. 46, 48.

[60] *New York Times,* "Closing Rally Vigorous," October 30, 1929, pp. 1-2.

[61] *New York Times,* "Transactions on the New York Stock Exchange, Tuesday, October 29, 1929," October 30, 1929, pp. 36, 39.

[62] *New York Times,* "Transactions on the New York Stock Exchange, Wednesday, November 13, 1929," November 14, 1929, pp. 40, 42.

[63] *New York Times,* "Argentina Aroused by Export of Gold," December 9, 1929, p. 48.

[64] *New York Times,* "Gold Office Closed, Argentine Peso Hit," December 18, 1929, p. 6.

[65] *New York Times,* "Argentina's Action on Gold Assailed," December 22, 1929, p. N7, N11.

[66] *New York Times,* "Yen is Near Par on a Gold Basis," January 12, 1930, pp. 41, 44.

[67] *New York Times,* "Bond Sales on the New York Stock Exchange, Thursday, April 10, 1930," April 11, 1930, p. 46.

[68] *New York Times,* "Transactions on the New York Stock Exchange, Thursday, April 17, 1930," April 18, 1930, pp. 39, 42.

[69] *New York Times,* "1,028 Economists Ask Hoover To Veto Pending Tariff Bill," May 5, 1930, pp. 1, 4.

[70] *New York Times,* "Changes in Tariff Rates Fixed in Hawley-Smoot Bill," June 15, 1930, pp. 26-27.

[71] *New York Times,* "Hoover Says He Will Sign Tariff Bill; Hails Flexible Clause as Giving Power to Correct Faults, End Foreign Protests," June 16, 1930, pp. 1-2.

[72] *New York Times,* "Democrats Turn Tariff Fire on Hoover as Senate Send Bill to White House; Break in Stock and Commodity Prices," June 17, 1930, pp. 1-2.

[73] *New York Times,* "Big Wheat Buying Mystifies Chicago," November 16, 1930, p. N15.

[74] *New York Times,* "Bond Sales on the New York Stock Exchange, Wednesday, December 17, 1930," December 18, 1930, pp. 36-37.

[75] *New York Times,* "July Wheat Falls, Lowest Since 1896," December 27, 1930, p. 26.

[76] *New York Times,* "1930 Stock Market Dealings," January 1, 1931, pp. 40-42.

[77] *New York Times,* "1930 Bond Market Dealings," January 1, 1931, pp. 43-46.

[78] *New York Times,* "Sharp Drop in 1930 in Foreign Trade," January 1, 1931, p. 46.

[79] *New York Times,* "Extra Session Foes Rely on President," January 3, 1931, p. 3.

[80] *New York Times,* "Definite Gain Seen in the Industries," Februay 10, 1931, p. 31.

[81] *New York Times,* "Topics in Wall Street," February 21, 1931, p. 26.

[82] *New York Times,* "Stocks Rise Briskly; 330 at New Highs," February 25, 1931, pp. 1, 5.

[83] *New York Times,* "Transactions on the New York Stock Exchange, Tuesday, February 24, 1931," February 25, 1931, pp. 39, 41.

[84] *New York Times,* "$10,000,000,000 Congress Quits; Vital Bills Lost by Filibuster in Senate," March 5, 1931, pp. 1, 18.

[85] *New York Times,* "71st Congress Set Peace-Time Spending Record With $10,249,819,215 Voted in Three Sessions," March 5, 1931, p. 18.

[86] *New York Times,* "Big Rail Bond Issues Sold in Two Hours," March 11, 1931, pp. 1, 3.

[87] *New York Times,* "Farm Board Warns that Wheat Buying Ends with 1930 Crop," March 23, 1931, pp. 1, 14.

[88] *New York Times,* "Flood of Selling Hits Wheat Market," March 24, 1931, p. 25.

[89] *New York Times,* "Wheat Prices Fall, Lowest Since 1895," March 24, 1931, p. 45.

[90] *New York Times,* "Topics in Wall Street," April 22, 1931, p. 37.

[91] *New York Times,* "Hoover Estimates a Cut of $315,799,083 in Federal Outlay," April 25, 1931, pp. 1-2.

[92] *New York Times,* "Borah Criticizes Hoover on Spending," April 30, 1931, pp. 1, 6.

[93] *New York Times,* "Home Bonds Reach 1931 Low Average," April 30, 1931, p. 34.

[94] *New York Times,* "Transactions on the New York Stock Exchange, Thursday, April 30, 1931," May 1, 1931, pp. 40, 42.

[95] *New York Times,* "Austria Acts to Save Biggest Private Bank," May 12, 1931, p. 21.

[96] *New York Times,* "World Bank's Aid Sought by Austria," May 13, 1931, p. 12.

[97] *New York Times,* "Bank Trouble Put Austria in Straits," May 13, 1931, p. 12.

[98] *New York Times,* "Austria Approves Credit Bank Loan," May 14, 1931, p. 8.

[99] *New York Times,* "Briand Condemns Union," May 17, 1931, p. 1.

[100] *New York Times,* "Vienna's Market Calm in Bank Crisis," May 18, 1931, p. 31.

[101] *New York Times,* "World Bank Offers Austria $14,000,000," May 19, 1931, pp. 1-2.

[102] *New York Times,* "Mr. Mellon on Taxes," May 25, 1931, p. 16.

[103] *New York Times,* "Capital is in Doubt on Seeking Tax Rise from New Congress," May 26, 1931, pp. 1, 4.

[104] *New York Times,* "Vienna Credit Bank Still in Need of Aid," May 27, 1931, p. 8.

[105] *New York Times,* "Austria Fights Off Financial Crash," May 28, 1931, p. 3.

[106] *New York Times,* "More Credit Bank Aid is Provided in Austria," May 29, 1931, p. 11.

[107] *New York Times,* "World Bank Grants Credit to Austria," May 30, 1931, p. 3.

[108] *New York Times,* "Financial Markets," May 31, 1931, p. N8.

[109] *New York Times,* "Reserve Banks Aid Austrian National," June 2, 1931, p. 48.

[110] *New York Times,* "Transactions on the New York Stock Exchange, Tuesday, June 2, 1931," June 3, 1931, pp. 40-41.

[111] *New York Times,* "Austria Raises Bank Rate to 6%," June 7, 1931, p. 29.

[112] *New York Times,* "Vienna Bank Crisis Laid to Paris Plot," June 7, 1931, p. E3.

[113] *New York Times,* "World Bank Opens Medium Loan Study," June 9, 1931, p. 12.

[114] *New York Times,* "12 Banks in Chain Closed in Chicago," June 10, 1931, p. 3.

[115] *New York Times,* "Reichsbank Raises Rate to End Drain," June 14, 1931, p. 2.

[116] *New York Times,* "French to Place New Vienna Bonds," June 14, 1931, p. 2.

[117] *New York Times,* "Paris Fears Abate on German Crisis," June 16, 1931, p. 12.

[118] *New York Times,* "Austrian National Bank Raises Rate," June 16, 1931, p. 12.

[119] *New York Times,* "Austrian Cabinet Quits on Bank Deal," June 17, 1931, p. 3.

[120] *New York Times,* "France Asks League to Aid Austrian Loan," June 17, 1931, p. 3.

[121] *New York Times,* "Salter Urges Plan to End Depression," June 17, 1931, p. 40.

[122] *New York Times,* "London Advances Austria $21,000,000," June 18, 1931, p. 4.

[123] *New York Times,* "Think British Loan has Saved Austria," June 19, 1931, p. 2.

[124] *New York Times,* "Contingent on Congress," June 21, 1931, pp. 1, 24.

[125] *New York Times,* "Cabinet in Austria Formed by Buresch," June 21, 1931, p. 26.

[126] *New York Times,* "Transactions on the New York Stock Exchange, Saturday, June 20, 1931," June 21, 1931, p. 38.

[127] *New York Times,* "Britain Hails Relief as a New Armistice," June 22, 1931, p. 15.

[128] *New York Times,* "Vienna Crisis Believed Over; London Bank's Action Pleases," June 22, 1931, p. 32.

[129] *New York Times,* "Says France Tried to Enchain Austria," June 25, 1931, p. 21.

[130] *New York Times,* "Germany Obtains $100,000,000 Credit," June 26, 1931, p. 19.

[131] *New York Times,* "Vienna Guarantees Bank's Home Debts," June 27, 1931, p. 8.

[132] *New York Times,* "Banks to the Rescue," June 27, 1931, p. 11.

[133] *New York Times,* "$70,000,000 of Credit Already Used by Reich," July 1, 1931, p. 20.

[134] *New York Times,* "Gain in Gold Here Largest Since War," July 1, 1931, p. 43.

[135] *New York Times,* "Reichsbank Delays Credit Restriction," July 5, 1931, p. 2.

[136] *New York Times,* "Draft of Accord Signed," July 7, 1931, p. 1.

[137] *New York Times,* "Reich to Seek Large Loan; Parley in London July 17; Italy Urges Arms Truce," July 9, 1931, pp. 1, 14.

[138] *New York Times,* "Loan of $400,000,000 is Sought by Luther in London and Paris," July 10, 1931, pp. 1, 10.

[139] *New York Times,* "German Banks Curb Runs by Depositors," July 14, 1931, p. 18.

[140] *New York Times,* "Cabinet Will Act Today," July 15, 1931, pp. 1, 16.

[141] *New York Times,* "American Loan Renewed," July 15, 1931, pp. 1, 17.

[142] *New York Times,* "Crisis Shuts Banks in Central Europe," July 15, 1931, pp. 1, 16.

[143] *New York Times,* "Washington Sees Reich Crisis Eased," July 15, 1931, p. 17.

[144] *New York Times,* "Germany Curbs Exchange; Red Riots Quickly Ended; Powers to Meet Monday," July 16, 1931, pp. 1, 16.

[145] *New York Times,* "Reich Crisis Upsets Exchange Markets," July 16, 1931, pp. 1, 17.

[146] *New York Times,* "55,000,000 Marks Paid Over by Reich," July 16, 1931, p. 16.

[147] *New York Times,* "Hungary Prepares Further Bank Curb," July 16, 1931, p. 23.

[148] *New York Times,* "Financial Markets," July 17, 1931, p. 27.

[149] *New York Times,* "Bankers Skeptical on New Aid to Reich," July 18, 1931, p. 5.

[150] *New York Times,* "No Currency Inflation," July 18, 1931, p. 6.

[151] *New York Times,* "Germany to Seize All Foreign Money," July 19, 1931, pp. 1, 18.

[152] *New York Times,* "Powers to Vote Aid to Reich Today; Taking Only Temporary Steps Now; Wall Street Doubts Success of Plan," July 23, 1931, pp. 1, 10.

[153] *New York Times,* "Bankruptcy Staved Off," July 24, 1931, pp. 1, 10.

[154] *New York Times,* "Wall Street Glum over Debt Meeting," July 24, 1931, p. 11.

[155] *New York Times,* "Wall St. Optimistic on German Outlook" July 26, 1931, p. N7, N13.

[156] *New York Times,* "Bankers to Leave Funds in Germany," July 30, 1931, pp. 1, 10.

[157] *New York Times,* "The Week in Europe; Michel Gets a Chance," August 2, 1931, p. E3.

[158] *New York Times,* "Cotton Price Crash on Huge Crop Report," August 11, 1931, pp. 1-2.

[159] *New York Times,* "Larger Wheat Yield Shown as of Aug. 1," August 11, 1931, p. 2.

[160] *New York Times,* "Loan Needed Immediately," August 24, 1931, pp. 1, 10.

[161] *New York Times,* "Wall Street Hails Credit for Britain," August 30, 1931, pp. N7, N10.

[162] *New York Times,* "Transactions on the New York Stock Exchange, Monday, August 31, 1931," September 1, 1931, p. 31.

[163] *New York Times,* "Bond Sales on the New York Stock Exchange, Monday, August 31, 1931," September 1, 1931, p. 35.

[164] *New York Times,* "Topics in Wall Street," September 2, 1931, p. 29.

[165] *New York Times,* "Financial Markets," September 3, 1931, p. 28.

[166] *New York Times,* "Transactions on the New York Stock Exchange, Wednesday, September 2, 1931," September 3, 1931, p. 27.

[167] *New York Times,* "Berlin Stocks Fall 25 to 40 Per Cent as Boerse Reopens," September 4, 1931, pp. 1,12.

[168] *New York Times,* "Topics in Wall Street," September 4, 1931, p. 26.

[169] *New York Times,* "Transactions on the New York Stock Exchange, Thursday, September 3, 1931," September 4, 1931, pp. 25, 27.

[170] *New York Times,* "Topics in Wall Street," September 5, 1931, p. 19.

[171] *New York Times,* "Our Gold Holdings Puzzle Economists," September 6, 1931, pp. 29, 32.

[172] *New York Times,* "Topics in Wall Street," September 9, 1931, p. 38.

[173] *New York Times,* "Topics in Wall Street," September 11, 1931, p. 28.

[174] *New York Times,* "Topics in Wall Street," September 12, 1931, p. 23.

[175] *New York Times,* "Commodity Prices Believed Stable," September 13, 1931, p. N9.

[176] *New York Times,* "No Early Recovery Here is Expected," September 14, 1931, p. 29.

[177] *New York Times,* "Topics in Wall Street," September 15, 1931, p. 32.

[178] *New York Times,* "Topics in Wall Street," September 17, 1931, p. 34.

[179] *New York Times,* "Financial Markets," September 19, 1931, p. 22.

[180] *New York Times,* "Topics in Wall Street," September 19, 1931, p. 23.

[181] *New York Times,* "Transactions on the New York Stock Exchange, Friday, September 18, 1931," September 19, 1931, pp. 22-23.

[182] *New York Times,* "Japanese Seize Mukden in Battle with Chinese; Rush More Troops to City," September 20, 1931, pp. 1, 8.

[183] *New York Times,* "Wave of Liquidation Hits London Market; Heavy Selling Here," September 20, 1931, pp. 1, 26.

[184] *New York Times,* "Bond Prices Slide in Heavy Trading," September 20, 1931, p. N10.

[185] *New York Times,* "Bond Sales on the New York Stock Exchange, Saturday, September 19, 1931," September 20, 1931, pp. N10-N11.

[186] *New York Times,* "Parliament to Back Move," September 21, 1931, p. 1.

[187] *New York Times,* "New York Bankers Confer," September 21, 1931, pp. 1-2.

[188] *New York Times,* "The British Government's Statement," September 21, 1931, p. 1.

[189] *New York Times,* "Geneva is Shocked by Crisis in London," September 21, 1931, pp. 1-2.

[190] *New York Times,* "Germany to Close All Boerses Today," September 21, 1931, pp. 1-2.

[191] *New York Times,* "Some Bankers Look to Revalorization," September 21, 1931, p. 3.

[192] *New York Times,* "Austria Restricts Exchange Dealings," September 24, 1931, p. 14.

[193] *New York Times,* "Sweden, Norway, Egypt Suspend Gold Standard; Others Likely to Follow," September 28, 1931, p. 1.

[194] *New York Times,* "$51,953,600 in Gold Lost to Us in a Day," September 29, 1931, p. 18.

[195] *New York Times,* "London Unemployed Riot Over Cut in Dole; Police Rout Mob Marching With Red Flag," October 1, 1931, p. 1.

[196] *New York Times,* "Transactions on the New York Stock Exchange, Wednesday, September 30, 1931," October 1, 1931, pp. 41, 43.

[197] *New York Times,* "Transactions on the New York Stock Exchange, Monday, October 5, 1931," October 6, 1931, pp. 36, 38.

[198] *New York Times,* "Bond Sales on the New York Stock Exchange, Monday, October 5, 1931," October 6, 1931, pp. 45-46.

[199] *New York Times,* "Broader Basis of Credit," October 7, 1931, p. 1.

[200] *New York Times,* "Financial Markets," October 7, 1931, p. 37.

[201] *New York Times,* "Transactions on the New York Stock Exchange, Tuesday, October 6, 1931," October 7, 1931, pp. 36, 39.

[202] *New York Times,* "Bond Sales on the New York Stock Exchange, Tuesday, October 6, 1931," October 7, 1931, pp. 38-39.

[203] *New York Times,* "Bank Rate at 2 1-2%; Stocks Rise Briskly," October 9, 1931, pp. 1, 17.

[204] *New York Times,* "Bank Rate Advanced to Combat Hoarding," October 16, 1931, pp. 1, 14.

[205] *New York Times,* "Washington Gratified by Britain's Payment," October 31, 1931, p. 8.

[206] *New York Times,* "Transactions on the New York Stock Exchange, Monday, November 9, 1931," November 10, 1931, pp. 38, 40.

[207] *New York Times,* "Bond Sales on the New York Stock Exchange, Monday, November 9, 1931," November 10, 1931, pp. 41-42.

[208] *New York Times,* "British Gold Action Held Unnecessary," November 19, 1931, p. 38.

[209] *New York Times,* "Foreign Exchange, Saturday, Dec. 12, 1931," December 13, 1931, p. N13.

[210] *New York Times,* "Gold Exports Forbidden," December 14, 1931, pp. 1, 4.

[211] *New York Times,* "Japan Suspends Gold Payments," December 15, 1931, p. 26.

[212] *New York Times,* "Hoover Says 'No Default' on Dec. 15 Debt Payments as Congress Debates Step," December 15, 1931, pp. 1-2.

[213] *New York Times,* "Clash Marks the Debate," December 19, 1931, pp. 1, 14.

[214] *New York Times,* "Sterling Off 10c as Franc Rallies," December 19, 1931, p. 32.

[215] *New York Times,* "Senate Ratifies Moratorium, 69 to 12, after Johnson Attack on President; Traylor Scores Hoover Credit Pool," December 23, 1931, pp. 1, 15.

[216] *New York Times,* "Opinions Conflict as Year Nears End," December 27, 1931, pp. 37, 40.

[217] *New York Times,* "1931 Record Shown by Business Index," December 31, 1931, p. 26.

[218] *New York Times,* "Chronological Record of the Outstanding Financial Events During the Past Year; The Story of 1931, Told by its Events," January 1, 1932, pp. 25-26.

[219] *New York Times,* "1931 Stock Market Dealings," January 1, 1932, pp. 37-39.

[220] *New York Times,* "1931 Bond Market Dealings," January 1, 1932, pp. 40-42.

[221] *New York Times,* "Britain to Repay on Tuesday Last of $200,000,000 Credit," April 3, 1932, p. N9.

[222] *New York Times,* "Senate Vote is 46 to 35," June 7, 1932, pp. 1, 14.

[223] *New York Times,* "Prepare New Rules to Collect Taxes," June 9, 1932, p. 31.

[224] *New York Times,* "France Withdraws Her Last Gold Here; Dollar Value Rises," June 15, 1932, pp. 1, 7.

[225] *New York Times,* "Transactions on the New York Stock Exchange, Friday, July 8, 1932," July 9, 1932, p. 20.

[226] *New York Times,* "Bond Sales on the New York Stock Exchange, Friday, July 8, 1932," July 9, 1932, p. 22.

[227] *New York Times,* "Business Index Recedes Slightly to New Low; Auto and Power Declines Offset Other Gains," August 21, 1932, p. F9.

[228] *New York Times,* "Cheered in Des Moines," October 5, 1932, pp. 1, 19.

[229] *New York Times,* "Hoover's Speech at Des Moines," October 5, 1932, pp. 18-19.

[230] *New York Times,* "5 Nations Default; Six Pay $98,686,910," December 16, 1932, p. 17.

[231] *New York Times,* "French Debt Note Given to Stimson," December 16, 1932, p. 16.

[232] *New York Times,* "Chronological Record of the Outstanding Financial Events of the Past Year" January 3, 1933, pp. 26-27.

[233] *New York Times,* "Weekly Business Index Advances to 57.5; Drop in Auto Output Offset by Other Gains," January 15, 1933, p. N15.

[234] *New York Times,* "Inflation as Cure Ridiculed by Bank," February 1, 1933, p. 25.

[235] *New York Times,* "Status of Banking Restrictions by States," March 4, 1933, p. F23.

[236] *New York Times,* "Status of Banking Restrictions by States," March 5, 1933, p. F24.

[237] *New York Times,* "Bank Bill is Enacted," March 10, 1933, pp. 1-2.

[238] *New York Times,* "Text of Emergency Banking Law Enacted as First Step in President Roosevelt's Program," March 10, 1933, p. 2.

[239] *New York Times,* "President Invokes Gold Hoarder Law," April 6, 1933, pp. 1, 7.

[240] *New York Times,* "President Takes Action," April 20, 1933, p. 1.

[241] *New York Times,* "New Order Issued to Turn In Gold," December 29, 1933, pp. 1-2.

[242] *New York Times,* "Taft? Hartley? The Names Ring a Bell, but Why?," November 16, 1987, p. B6.

[243] *New York Times,* "Futures, Thursday, January 25 2001," January 26, 2001, p. C11.

[244] *New York Times,* steel production estimates, January 5, 1928 to December 17, 1931.

[245] *New York Times,* Chicago, Minneapolis, and Winnipeg grain prices, January 7, 1928 to December 25, 1931. Prices are for Friday or last non-holiday prior to Friday of each week.

[246] *New York Times,* Averages of 40 domestic and 10 foreign government issue bonds, January 5, 1929 to December 31, 1932. Averages are for Friday or last non-holiday prior to Friday of each week.

[247] *New York Times,* weekly car loadings reports from American Railway Association, February 4, 1931 to February 3, 1932.

[248] *New York Times,* "Foreign Exchange," July 4, 1931 to January 31, 1934. Rates are for Friday or last non-holiday prior to Friday of each week.

[249] Noyes, Alexander D., "The Course of the Depression and the Signs of a Turn," *New York Times,* October 30, 1932, p. XX3.

[250] Noyes, Alexander D., "Inflation Versus Sound Money: The Past and Present," *New York Times,* March 5, 1933, p. XX3.

[251] Rand, Ayn. *Atlas Shrugged.* 1957. Reprint, New York, NY: Plume, 1999.
Excerpt available at http://www.capitalismmagazine.com/index.php?news=1826 (Francisco's Money Speech).

[252] Reuters, "FACTBOX–Ten worst months for the Dow and S&P 500," October 31, 2008.
Available at http://www.reuters.com/article/idUSN3136880620081031. Retrieved August 3, 2010.

[253] Robbins, Lionel. *The Great Depression.* 1934. Reprint, Auburn, AL: Ludwig von Mises Institute, 2007.

[254] Rothbard, Murray. *America's Great Depression,* 5th ed. Auburn, AL: Ludwig von Mises Institute, 2000. Reprinted 2008.

[255] Rothbard, Murray. *What Has Government Done to Our Money?* 5th ed. and *The Case for a 100 Percent Gold Dollar,* 2nd ed. Auburn, AL: Ludwig von Mises Institute, 2005.

[256] Shirer, William L. *The Rise and Fall of the Third Reich.* New York, NY: Simon and Schuster, 1959.

[257] Skousen, W. Cleon. *The 5000 Year Leap.* USA: National Center for Constitutional Studies, 2006.

[258] Tanner, Michael D. *Leviathan on the Right: How Big-Government Conservatism Brought Down the Republican Revolution.* Washington, DC: Cato Institute, 2007.

[259] Tax Foundation, "U.S. Federal Individual Income Tax Rates History, 1913-2010," December 31, 2009.
Available at http://www.taxfoundation.org/publications/show/151.html. Retrieved February 5, 2010.

[260] *Time,* "Austria: Black Week," June 8, 1931.
Available at http://www.time.com/time/magazine/article/0,9171,741788,00.html.

[261] Time Magazine, Editors. *Time: Almanac 2009.* Chicago, IL: Time, 2008.

[262] Vernon, J.R. "The 1920-21 Deflation: the Role of Aggregate Supply," *Economic Inquiry,* Vol. 29, No. 3, July 1991, pp. 572-580.
Available at http://www.accessmylibrary.com. Retrieved July 20, 2010.

[263] Wikipedia, "Argentine peso moneda nacional," 2010.
Available at http://en.wikipedia.org/wiki/Argentine_peso_moneda_nacional. Retrieved July 23, 2010.

[264] Wikipedia, "Austro-Hungarian krone," 2010.
Available at http://en.wikipedia.org/wiki/Austro-Hungarian_krone. Retrieved July 23, 2010.

[265] Wikipedia, "Canadian dollar," 2010.
Available at http://en.wikipedia.org/wiki/Canadian_dollar.
Retrieved July 23, 2010.

[266] Wikipedia, "Dutch guilder," 2010.
Available at http://en.wikipedia.org/wiki/Dutch_guilder. Retrieved July 23, 2010.

[267] Wikipedia, "Japanese currency," 2010.
Available at http://en.wikipedia.org/wiki/Japanese_currency.
Retrieved July 23, 2010.

[268] Wikipedia, "Russian ruble," 2010.
Available at http://en.wikipedia.org/wiki/Russian_ruble. Retrieved July 23, 2010.

[269] Wikipedia, "Scandinavian Monetary Union," 2010.
Available at http://en.wikipedia.org/wiki/Scandinavian_Monetary_Union. Retrieved July 23, 2010.

[270] Wikipedia, "Vereinsthaler," 2010.
Available at http://en.wikipedia.org/wiki/Vereinsthaler. Retrieved July 23, 2010.

[271] Word IQ, "Russian ruble – Definition," 2010.
Available at http://www.wordiq.com/definition/Russian_ruble.
Retrieved July 23, 2010.

NOTE: Page numbers for the *New York Times* articles are those provided by the ProQuest Historical Newspapers database. In some cases, the page numbers for these articles in the microfilm records of the *New York Times* are different.

About the Author

Eric H. Allen received his PhD in Electrical Engineering from the Massachusetts Institute of Technology in 1998. His doctoral thesis work involved the study of independent generator decision-making in electricity markets. Eric is currently employed in the analysis of electric power systems (which, like the economy, are large, complex dynamic systems).